Churchill

An Illustrated Life

Churchill
An Illustrated Life

BRENDA RALPH LEWIS

METRO BOOKS
New York

METRO BOOKS
New York

An Imprint of Sterling Publishing
387 Park Avenue South
New York, NY 10016

Editorial and design by
Amber Books Ltd
74–77 White Lion Street
London N1 9PF
www.amberbooks.co.uk

Project Editor: James Bennett
Design: Jerry Williams
Picture Research: Terry Forshaw

ISBN: 978-1-4351-4655-6

Contents

INTRODUCTION

If Winston Churchill had died in his forties, which he believed was the lifespan for males in his aristocratic family, he would have gone down in history as a brilliant but maverick failure. Instead, Churchill defied the statistics to live another 50 years and earned a unique place in British and world history.

The difference between these two destinies lay within a short period of time: the five years of World War II, between 1940 and 1945, when Churchill was British Prime Minister and most of western Europe was occupied by Nazi Germany. Long before this, Churchill had recognised the threat the Nazis, and their leader Adolf Hitler, posed to peace and took every opportunity to impress the sombre truth on pacifist British governments intent on appeasing Hitler rather than confronting him. Over and over again, Churchill called for immediate rearmament to counter the military build-up in Nazi Germany. His warnings were ignored and he was sidelined by other politicians, who regarded him as an eccentric political irritant.

Churchill was a man born out of his time. Even in his younger days, thirsting for glory and not fussy about how he acquired it, he was regarded as a troublemaker. He was an atypical aristocrat who relished popular acclaim, an ambitious opportunist and a self-publicist who promoted himself in pushy, 'un-English' ways.

Churchill's stand against appeasement in the 1930s earned him a further label – warmonger. These were Churchill's 'wilderness years' when he was out of office and out of favour. Like the mythical Cassandra, his predictions, though accurate, seemed fated to go unheeded. But fate proved kinder to Churchill than it had to

Churchill (above) early in his political career. Churchill was well equipped to be a politician. Although short in stature, he made up for it with resounding speeches delivered in majestic language and with an air of total confidence. As Minister of Munitions, Churchill (right) visited Lille in October 1918, towards the end of World War I. That night, a German aircraft dropped a large bomb in the street near the house where he was staying. He emerged unscathed.

the ancient Greek heroine. The outbreak of war with Germany in September 1939 demonstrated how right Churchill had been and how mistaken the British government's policy of appeasement was. Churchill became Prime Minister in May 1940 and within weeks Britain was in a desperate situation, with Nazi forces across the English Channel poised to invade. Even as he took office, Churchill left the people of Britain in no doubt about the grim future they had to face. 'I have nothing to offer but blood, toil, tears and sweat. We have before us an ordeal of the most grievous kind,' he told Parliament on 13 May. 'We have before us many,

During World War II Churchill inspired the British people with his defiance. He regularly toured the areas damaged by bombing and praised the 'tough fibre' of Londoners whose homes and businesses had been destroyed.

Churchill's state funeral on 30 January, 1965, was only the fourth accorded to a non-royal. During his lying-in-state more than 350,000 people queued to pay their last respects.

many long months of struggle and of suffering. You ask, what is our policy? I can say: it is to wage war by sea, land and air, with all our might and with all the strength that God can give us; to wage war against a monstrous tyranny, never surpassed in the dark, lamentable catalogue of human crime. You ask, what is our aim? I can answer in one word: it is victory, victory at all costs, victory in spite of all terror, victory, however long and hard the road may be; for without victory, there is no survival.'

This impassioned appeal to patriotism and courage stirred the people of Britain. Churchill's speeches during those dark weeks were emotional and uncompromising, and typified the 'bulldog spirit' he came to be identified with.

Churchill himself regarded his leadership of Britain during World War II as no more than his allotted destiny. His whole life, he felt, had been a preparation for this 'finest hour', when he would walk with that destiny. There was already a strong hint of Churchill's future place in history in 1889, when he was still only 15 and a schoolboy at Harrow. His parents and teachers saw a troublesome boy, always in some scrape or other, and seemingly unable to behave. Murland Evans, an older fellow pupil, saw something entirely different. 'Like other boys at Harrow,' Evans remembered, 'I was greatly attracted by this extraordinary boy. His commanding intelligence, his bravery, charm and indifference to ugly surroundings, vivid imagination, descriptive powers, general knowledge of the world and of history – gained no one knew how, but never disputed – and above all that magnetism and sympathy which shone in his eyes and radiated from a personality which – even under the severe repression of our public school system – dominated great numbers around him, many of whom were his superiors in age and prowess.'

This book tells the story of how Churchill the boy travelled a long, frustrating road before his destiny came true, and how Churchill the man, once regarded as a misfit and a maverick, believed he was marked for greatness and proved himself right.

YOUNG WINSTON

WINSTON CHURCHILL WAS BORN TO PRIVILEGE AND HIGH SOCIAL STANDING, BUT HIS WAS NOT A HAPPY CHILDHOOD. NEGLECTED BY HIS PARENTS, AT SEVEN HE WAS SENT TO A SCHOOL WHICH SPECIALISED IN RUTHLESS DISCIPLINE AND BEATINGS. HE WAS 20 BEFORE HE ESCAPED THIS DEPRESSING EXISTENCE, WHEN HE ENTERED SANDHURST TO TRAIN FOR A MILITARY CAREER.

IN KEEPING WITH THE PATTERN of his long and often turbulent life, it was typical of Winston Leonard Spencer Churchill that his entry into the world should be both hurried and dramatic. He arrived two months early, on 30 November, 1874, at Blenheim Palace, the property of his grandfather, John Winston Spencer Churchill, the seventh Duke of Marlborough.

Blenheim was not supposed to be Winston's birthplace. His father, Lord Randolph, the Duke's third son, had planned the birth to take place in London. The house he had chosen and rented for the purpose, in fashionable Charles Street, Mayfair, was conveniently close to the best obstetric practices in the country as well as the society haunts Lord Randolph frequented.

These arrangements were disrupted when Winston's American mother, the former Jennie Jerome, suffered a fall on 24 November while walking with a hunt in the Oxfordshire countryside. Four days later, despite Lord Randolph's attempts to dissuade her, the wilful Jennie went for a drive over rough country in a pony trap.

Blenheim Palace (left), Churchill's birthplace, was built in the early 1700s near Woodstock in Oxfordshire. One of Britain's grandest stately homes, its great hall features a remarkable painted ceiling depicting Churchill's ancestor, the first Duke of Marlborough, victorious in battle.
The infant Winston (above) with his mother Jennie. The pose suggests a fond relationship, but in reality Lady Randolph was a neglectful mother.

The jolting triggered premature labour and Winston was born the next day, long before the London obstetrician Lord Randolph had retained could reach Blenheim.

Winston's parents were newlyweds, married only seven months, and they had known each other for only seven months before that. Lord Randolph met Jennie Jerome on 12 August, 1873, at a shipboard party during the Cowes regatta, off the Isle of Wight. Jennie was the 20-year-old daughter of Leonard Jerome, part-owner of the *New York Times* and a speculator who had made a fortune from horse racing. She was beautiful, shapely and spirited and Lord Randolph was instantly smitten. The feeling was mutual and the couple became engaged three days later.

Leonard Jerome was impressed that his daughter had landed such an illustrious catch as the son of an English duke. The Marlboroughs belonged to a powerful and influential elite, the landowning aristocracy who dominated British political, financial and social life. The Marlborough dynasty had begun with John Churchill, the first Duke who was considered to be one of Britain's greatest military leaders. John Churchill made his reputation between 1704 and 1709, with his four victories over the French and their allies during the War of the Spanish Succession. The first of these triumphs, at Blenheim in Bavaria, southern Germany, gave its name to the magnificent palace built for Marlborough as a sign of the country's gratitude. For Leonard Jerome, the social cachet of a connection between his family and the scions of the British nobility was considerable, and he approved the match.

'SPORTING AND VULGAR'

Lord Randolph's father was not so sure. He was doubtful whether his son's importunate passion for Jennie would last, and he was equally concerned about her father's credentials. 'This Mr J,' he said, 'seems to be a sporting and, I should think, vulgar kind of man … he has been bankrupt twice, and may be so again.'

John Churchill, founder of the Marlborough dynasty, was given the title of duke in 1702, the year in which his long-term patron, Queen Anne, was crowned.

His own family history told the seventh Duke a great deal about financial insecurity. Despite his title, the Duke came from a long line of profligates whose extravagant habits led to ruin several times. So it was hardly surprising that the Duke was concerned about the financial arrangements 'this Mr J' meant to make for Jennie. This was not his only worry. In English law, a married woman's property was controlled by her husband. But Leonard Jerome had more egalitarian, American ideas: as far as he was concerned, a married woman's property was her own.

PARIS WEDDING

After months of tussling a compromise was reached: the capital of £50,000 offered by Jerome, producing an income of £2000 a year, would be shared equally between husband and wife. The Duke contributed another £1100 a year for life, settled on Lord Randolph, so the couple could look forward to an income of over £150,000 a year at today's values.

The marriage took place on 15 April, 1874, on neutral ground. It was no grand society wedding. Lord Randolph and Jennie were married at the British embassy in Paris, before a few witnesses who included the bride's parents, but no Duke and Duchess. Instead, the Marlboroughs were represented by Lord Randolph's elder brother George, Marquis of Blandford.

In February 1874, Lord Randolph had narrowly secured election as Member of Parliament for Woodstock, traditionally a Marlborough family seat, but in 1884 it disappeared when 'family' constituencies were abolished. Lord Randolph soon arranged to change constituency and remained in Parliament. By that time the 12-year-old Winston had discovered a sombre truth about his father. Lord Randolph was too caught up with the pressures

Sarah Jennings married John Churchill in 1677 and became the first Duchess of Marlborough in 1702. As the favourite of Queen Anne, the strong-minded Sarah used her influence to secure her husband's title.

and excitements of politics to have much time, thought or effort to spare for parenthood.

Churchill's childhood experiences made him in later years acutely aware of the need to engage with his own children. The contrast between Lord Randolph and Winston as fathers was highlighted by a comment made after dinner by Winston to his own son, also named Randolph, in 1938. Relations between father and son were not always congenial, due mainly to young Randolph's extravagance and fierce temper. Even so, the meal was a pleasant encounter. Towards the end of it, Winston told Randolph: 'We have this evening had a longer period of continuous conversation together than the total which I ever had with my father in the whole course of his life.'

The gulf between parent and child which Churchill recalled with such wistful regret was not unusual in aristocratic

Winston's father, Lord Randolph Churchill, died at the age of 46 in 1895, probably of syphilis. The disease was a taboo subject in Victorian society and a disgrace on any family.

families of the late Victoria era. Children were often regarded as intrusions in their parents' lives and consigned to the nursery for long periods. Churchill later wrote of his mother Jennie: 'She shone for me like the evening star. I loved her dearly – but at a distance.'

As with many nobly born boys of his time, Churchill had a warm and close relationship with his nurse, Mrs Elizabeth Everest, to whom he gave the pet name of 'Woom' or 'Womanny'. The letters they exchanged while Winston was at school were intensely affectionate. 'My darling Winny,' Everest would begin, ending with 'Lots of love and kisses, From your loving old Woom'. 'My darling old Woom,' young Winston would reply, closing with 'Good Bye darling … with love from Winny'.

'HATEFUL SERVITUDE'

At the age of six or seven, boys from aristocratic families were sent away to boarding school. Winston entered his first school, St George's near Ascot in Berkshire, in 1882, and later painted it as a place of suffering and terror. 'How I hated this school and what a life of anxiety I lived for more than two years,' he wrote. ' … I counted the days and the hours to the end of every term, when I should return home from this hateful servitude.'

According to Churchill, the boys at St George's lived in the shadow of the birch. The headmaster, using all his strength, would flay a miscreant's bottom 20 times or more. Other boys, awaiting similar punishment, shook with fear as they listened to the screams coming from the headmaster's study. Winston was himself flogged after stealing sugar from the

Jennie, Lady Randolph Churchill, was a beautiful and brilliant member of the aristocratic social scene. Her glittering social life took up much of her time, to the detriment of her sons.

school pantry. His reaction was defiant. Once the punishment was over, he snatched the headmaster's straw hat from its hook behind a door, and kicked it to pieces in a rage.

Boys were often miserable and lonely at school, and desperate for parental visits. Winston repeatedly begged his mother Jennie to visit him at St George's, but after taking him to the school on his first day, she failed to return.

CHILDHOOD AILMENTS

The reception was cool when Winston arrived for his first holiday from St George's at his parents' London house, 2 Connaught Place, on the north side of Hyde Park. His school report had been poor. Winston was bottom in his class of eleven. He was persistently late, and was 'a constant trouble to everybody and … always in some scrape or other. He cannot be trusted to behave himself anywhere.' Later in life, Churchill commented laconically: 'I was what grown up people in their offhand way called "a troublesome boy".' Winston was scarcely less trouble at home where his brother John, known as Jack, born in 1880, became his prime target.

Winston teased Jack without mercy, causing screams, tears and uproar in the nursery.

Winston was not a robust child. He was narrow-chested, with a rather puny physique. Even as an adult, he stood no more than 1m 67cm (5ft 6in) tall. His most arresting features were his eyes, full of humour with more than a hint of mischief. But his chalky pale complexion gave him a sickly look. He was often unwell and suffered a series of childhood ailments. In 1884, Dr Robson Roose, the Churchill family physician, suggested that he would be better off in a more healthy climate by the seaside. Winston's parents took Dr Roose's advice. To Winston's great relief, they removed him from St George's and sent him to a school in Brighton run by the Misses Thomson.

The Thomsons ran a less punitive regime than St George's, but failed to produce an improvement in Winston's behaviour. He had obviously been troublesome at home during the Christmas holidays of 1884, for after returning to Brighton, the ten-year-old boy wrote bitterly to his mother, 'You must be happy without me, no screams from Jack or complaints. It must be heaven on earth.'

> **'…a constant trouble to everybody and … always in some scrape or other. He cannot be trusted to behave himself anywhere.'**
>
> CHURCHILL'S SCHOOL REPORT

CHURCHILL ON THE ENGLISH ARISTOCRACY

English Society still existed in its old form. It was a brilliant and powerful body …. The few hundred great families who had governed England for so many generations and had seen her rise to the pinnacle of her glory, were inter-related to an enormous extent by marriage …. The leading figures of Society were in many cases the leading statesmen in Parliament and also the leading sportsmen on the Turf. Lord Salisbury was accustomed scrupulously to avoid calling a Cabinet when there was racing at Newmarket and the House of Commons made a practice of adjourning for the (racing at) Derby. Glittering house parties … comprised all the elements which made a gay and splendid social circle in close relation to the business of Parliament, the hierarchies of the Army and Navy and the policy of the State …

Nº. 28,176.

BIRTHS.

On the 30th Nov., at Blenheim Palace, the Lady RANDOLPH CHURCHILL, prematurely, of a son.

On the 7th Oct., at Rangoon, the wife of HALKETT F. JACKSON, Esq., Lieut. and Adjutant 67th Regt., of a daughter.

On the 20th Oct., at Bombay, the wife of Capt. G. W. OLDHAM, R.E., of a son.

On the 27th Oct., at Ranchi, Chota Nagpore, the wife of Capt. NINIAN LOWIS, B.S.C., Assistant Commissioner, of a daughter.

On the 6th Nov., 1874, at Belgaum, India, the wife of J. CHARLES M. PIGOTT, Esq., Lieut. 66th Regt., of a daughter.

On the 20th Nov., at Marlborough-terrace, Roath, Cardiff, the wife of THOMAS J. ALLEN, of a daughter.

On the 21st Nov., the wife of POYNTZ WRIGHT, M.R.C.S.E., of a daughter.

On the 22d Nov., at South-hill-park, Hampstead, the wife of ALBERT STRAUBE, of a son.

On the 26th Nov., at Wolfang, Queensland, Australia, the wife of HENRY DE SATGÉ, Esq., of a son.

On the 27th Nov., at Wolverton House, Bucks, the wife of SPENCER R. HARRISON, Esq., of a daughter.

On the 28th Nov., at Eton College, the wife of ARTHUR C. JAMES, Esq., of a daughter.

On the 28th Nov., at Churt Vicarage, near Farnham, the wife of the Rev. A. B. ALEXANDER, of a daughter.

On the 29th Nov., at 31, Spencer-square, Ramsgate, the wife of Mr. GEO. HAWKINS, late of Brighton, of a son.

On the 29th Nov., at Kibworth Beauchamp, Leicestershire, the wife of THOMAS MACAULAY, Surgeon, of a daughter.

On the 29th Nov., at Nunthorpe Grove, York, Mrs. WOOD CLARKE, of a son.

On the 29th Nov., at Oakbraes, Godalming, the wife of Major A. OLIVER RUTHERFURD, of a son.

On the 29th Nov., at 80, rue Royale, Tours, the wife of Monsieur ALFRED HAINGUERLOT, of a son.

On the 30th Nov., at 10, Talbot-road, Westbourne-park, W., the wife of V. C. DE RIVAZ, of a daughter.

On the 30th Nov., at Bayfield, Southsea, the wife of L. HOLLAND REIDE, of a son.

Winston Churchill's birth was announced in The Times in 1874. It was a measure of the high status of the family that the announcement appeared at the top of the Births column, whereas other announcements were printed in date order.

Winston was being eased back into school lessons, he began to enjoy his education, and for the first time, revealed some of his intellectual strengths:

'I got gradually much stronger in that bracing air and gentle surroundings,' he wrote. 'I was allowed to learn things which interested me: French, history, lots of poetry by heart and above all riding and swimming. The impression of those years makes a pleasant picture in my mind, in contrast to my earlier schoolday memories.'

Winston was by now an excited observer of his father's successful parliamentary career. In 1885, Lord Randolph had become Secretary for India, and in 1886 Chancellor of the Exchequer. But success had its drawbacks. Lord Randolph's ascent to the Chancellorship, the second most exalted government office, put an end to the interest he had shown in his son during his illness. In mid November 1886, Winston was writing mournfully: 'You never came to see me on Sunday when you were in Brighton'. Lord Randolph had not visited his son on an earlier trip, either.

Despite the neglect he suffered, Winston was immensely proud of his father and, in his youthful way, he romanticised Lord Randolph. But he did not realise that his father was in reality a disruptive presence in Parliament. Even his own Prime Minister, Lord Salisbury, described Lord Randolph as unstable, juvenile and untamed. Lord Randolph was unpopular with other ministers too. His first budget included spending cuts on armaments and was

BRIGHTON SCHOOLDAYS

Unfortunately, Winston's move to Brighton did not appear to have the desired effect on his health. In March 1886 he fell seriously ill with pneumonia, an illness which often recurred in his later life. His parents, fearing he might die, rushed down to the seaside town to be with him. The crisis lasted for three days before they could be sure he was going to survive. Winston's convalescence took several months and it was July before he was able to resume school. Meanwhile, his father, seriously frightened by his son's apparent brush with death, gave him some of the attention he had wanted for so long. Lord Randolph came to visit Winston bringing a present of grapes and in April he arrived with a toy steam engine. In the summer, when

WINSTON CHURCHILL
WAS BORN PREMATURELY
IN THIS UNADORNED BED
IN A SMALL GROUND
FLOOR ROOM AT
BLENHEIM PALACE IN
1874, AFTER A 24-HOUR
LABOUR. BOTH MOTHER
AND CHILD WERE LUCKY
TO SURVIVE, FOR
CHILDBIRTH IN THE LATE
19TH CENTURY WAS STILL
DANGEROUS AND
PREMATURE INFANTS
GENERALLY HAD POOR
PROSPECTS.

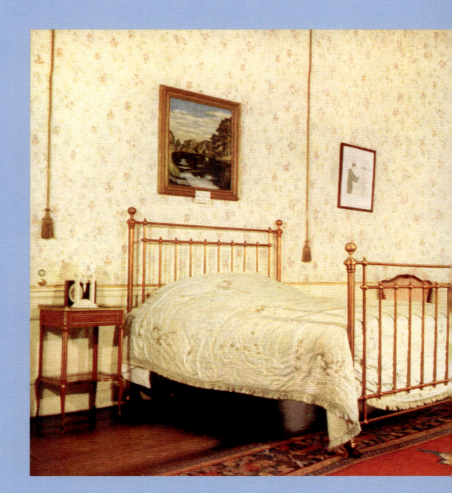

In 1764, Lancelot 'Capability' Brown set out Blenheim's gardens complete with lakes and water terraces, creating 'the finest view in England', as Lady Randolph Churchill once boasted. Blenheim Palace has been the country seat of the Marlborough family for 11 generations.

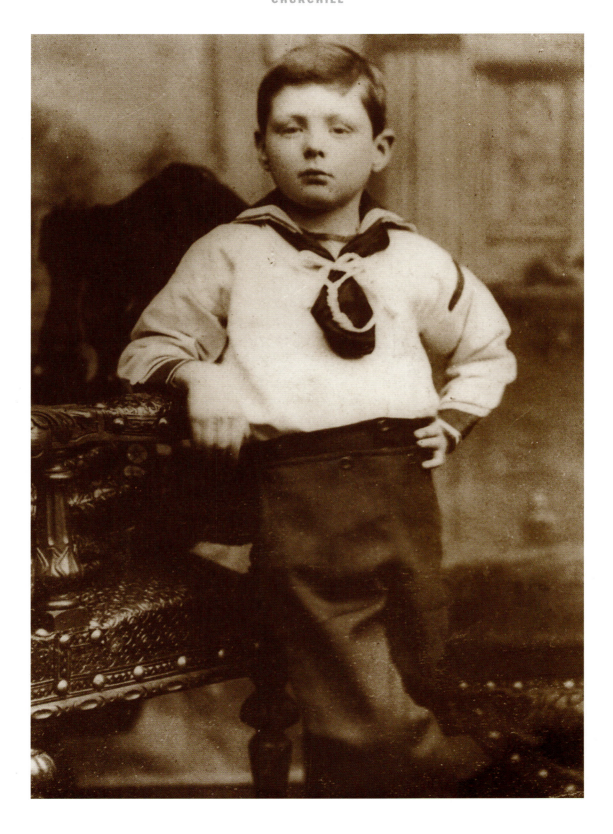

Winston was around six years old when this picture was taken in 1881. The sailor suit he is wearing was a popular alternative to formal dress for boys until well into the 20th century.

sabotaged by the First Lord of the Admiralty and the Secretary of State for War, both of whom had a vested interest in spending on military hardware. Lord Randolph, enraged, wrote to Lord Salisbury tendering his resignation, claiming that he was doing so to avoid 'wrangling and quarrelling in the Cabinet'. It was all a bluff. He was sure the Prime Minister would ask him to stay on, but he was wrong. Lord Salisbury saw his chance to get rid of a nuisance and took it. Having effectively destroyed his own career, Lord Randolph never held political office again.

Winston believed that Lord Salisbury was motivated by jealousy of his young and brilliant father. Two months later, in February 1887, Winston was with Jennie at a pantomime in Brighton when an on-stage representation of Lord Randolph was loudly booed. Winston burst into tears and rounded furiously on a man who was hissing from the seat behind him. 'Stop that row,' Winston demanded, 'You ... you snub-nosed Radical!' When Jennie told him of the incident, Lord Randolph was pleased at the way his son had come to his defence and rewarded Winston with a valuable gold sovereign.

PUBLIC SCHOOL LIFE

Winston's record was now showing a marked improvement on the standard of his early school years, when he had often been bottom of the class. By November 1887, when he had turned 13 and was preparing to move on to Harrow, one of Britain's oldest and most distinguished public schools, he was a boy transformed. In that year's examinations at the Misses Thomson's school, he came first in English history, algebra, ancient history and Bible history, and second in geography and arithmetic.

Winston's knowledge of Greek was improving and he won two prizes at school, for English and Scripture.

During the examinations, in a rare show of paternal interest, Lord Randolph came down to Brighton and took Winston out to tea. The boy was delighted. The unexpected treat encouraged him – prematurely as it turned out – to look ahead to a Christmas party at home where he and his friends would be entertained by a conjurer, doubling as a ventriloquist. But Winston's hopes were dashed when his parents announced that they planned to spend the Christmas period in Russia and would not return to England until February.

Winston, deeply disappointed, was farmed out for Christmas, with his brother Jack, to their Marlborough grandmother at Blenheim Palace. Afterwards, back in London, they stayed with their aunt, Lily, Duchess of Marlborough, whose husband, Lord Randolph's elder brother, had succeeded to the dukedom in 1883. Despite efforts to keep the brothers entertained, this was a miserable time for them. 'We feel so destitute,' a mournful Winston wrote to Jennie.

Before long, Winston was distracted by the impending entrance examinations to Harrow. The prospect filled him with trepidation, but he passed the examination and went up to Harrow in April 1888. A month later, he joined the school cadet force. Soon, he was learning to

CHURCHILL ON SCHOOL LESSONS

My teachers saw me at once backward and precocious, reading books beyond my years and yet at the bottom of the form. They were offended. They had large resources of compulsion at their disposal, but I was stubborn. Where my reason, imagination or interest were not engaged, I would not or I could not learn.

shoot with a Martini-Henry rifle which was then in service with the army. There were regular drills and a mock battle staged at Haileybury School in Hertfordshire, where Winston was charged with carrying cartridges. Although the Harrow cadet force lost the battle and was obliged to withdraw, Winston found the experience thrilling. He had always been interested in the army and, at home, had built up a collection of 1500 toy soldiers which he carefully arranged in correct battle order. Years later, he remembered his father visiting his 'battlefield' and carefully studying the scene for some 20 minutes.

'At the end,' Winston wrote, 'he asked me if I would like to go into the army. I thought it would be splendid to command an army, so I said "Yes" at once – and immediately I was taken at my word.'

Later, Winston discovered that his father's interest was not all it appeared to be. Despite the excitements of the Harrow cadet force, Winston was thinking of going to university to study law. Lord Randolph had different ideas.

CHURCHILL ON SCHOOL EXAMINATIONS

I had scarcely passed my twelfth birthday when I entered the inhospitable regions of examinations, through which for the next seven years I was destined to journey. These examinations were a great trial to me. The subjects which were dearest to the examiners were almost invariably those I fancied least. I would have liked to (be) examined in history, poetry and writing essays. The examiners on the other hand, were partial to Latin and mathematics .... Moreover, the questions ... they asked on both these subjects were almost invariably those to which I was unable to suggest a satisfactory answer .... When I would have willingly displayed my knowledge, they sought to expose my ignorance. This sort of treatment had only one result: I did not do well at examinations.

'For years,' Winston later commented, 'I thought my father, with his experience and flair, had discerned in me the qualities of military genius. But I was later told that he had only come to the conclusion that I was not clever enough to go to the Bar.'

The results Winston was achieving at Harrow tended to contradict this judgement. Although his behaviour still left much to be desired – he was criticised for being forgetful, careless, unpunctual and even slovenly – he was bright enough to perform a prodigious feat of memory: reciting by heart a thousand lines from *The Lays of Ancient Rome* by Thomas Babington Macaulay. For this, he won a special prize and, in addition, received the history prize in two consecutive terms during 1888. The same year, he also came first in Roman history. Learning Greek had once been the greatest bugbear in Winston's young life, but at Harrow he did well in both Latin and Greek.

It seemed plain that here was an awakening intellect of promise, but Lord Randolph did not perceive this or, if he did, he ignored it. He insisted that his son be transferred to the army class at Harrow so that he could prepare, in time, to enter a military academy. Winston had no option but to obey and took the examination for entry into the class. He did badly in mathematics and the result closed another door for him: it was unlikely he would be able to go on to the Woolwich military academy where future officers in the Royal Artillery and the Royal Engineers were trained. Instead, it had to be the less prestigious Sandhurst, and a future as an infantry or cavalry officer.

PREPARING FOR THE ARMY

Winston wrote to his mother that the army class was a bore, and spoiled his half-term breaks with extra work. For solace, he turned to books and became a keen reader, with a particular interest in history. He also had a stroke of good fortune: Robert Somervell, who taught Winston English, had great enthusiasm for his subject and a flair for communicating it to his pupils. Winston,

whose future impact in politics depended so much on his majestic command of English, learned much from Somervell including, as he later wrote, 'the essential structure of the ordinary British sentence – which is a noble thing.'

But the everyday grind of the Army class still taxed him. He resented the way it impinged on the subjects he found most interesting, such as history and English. He also hated one of the mandatory subjects – German – and never quite managed to get his tongue round it. In 1890, two years after entering Harrow, Winston faced his impending army preliminary examination with some anxiety. Once again, his fears were groundless. He passed in all subjects, helped by an extraordinary stroke of luck. The geography examination included questions on a particular country, but no one knew in advance which one it would be. Winston took a chance, picked New Zealand out of a possible 25, and revised it thoroughly. On the day, he opened the geography paper and, to his delight, found that New Zealand was the first question.

Winston turned 16 ten days before the army examination. On a short visit to London, he discovered girls and attempted to 'make an impression on pretty Miss Weaslet', only to be abruptly hauled away for the journey home. Another of Winston's adolescent discoveries was smoking. His mother tried to get him to give up by telling him 'how foolish and how silly you look doing it'. Afterwards, she bribed her son by promising to get Lord Randolph to give him 'a gun and a pony'. Winston gave in and agreed to give up smoking 'for at least six months'.

In 1884, Churchill turned 10. Two weeks after his birthday, a boy at school stabbed him in the chest with a penknife, drawing blood. The school authorities blamed the other boy, who had a fierce temper, but it seems that Winston began the trouble by pulling the boy's ear.

Mrs Everest also continued to treat Winston like a child and sent him motherly advice not to keep a candle burning by his bedside at night and not to walk too close to the edge of railway

Churchill's mother, Jennie, was a glamorous socialite. An admirer once said that there was 'more of the panther than the woman in her look'. She remarried twice after Lord Randolph's death, in 1900 and 1918, to men considerably younger than herself.

platforms. In 1891, Jennie, who decided that Winston was too grown up to need a nurse any more, decided to dismiss Mrs Everest. Winston and Jack became very upset and Winston protested vigorously at the prospect of losing his beloved 'Womanny'. Ultimately, Jennie had to make a special arrangement for Mrs Everest to work at the London home of their Marlborough grandmother in Grosvenor Square, so that Winston and Jack could still see her.

JUVENILE JAPES

Later in the same year, Winston proved that he was still prone to juvenile japes. That summer, he was out walking with a group of other Harrow boys when they came across a derelict factory. Most of its windows had been destroyed and the boys decided to finish the job. The noise of smashing glass attracted the attention of the watchman, who reported the miscreants to the school. As punishment, Winston and others received a 'swishing' – schoolboy slang for a caning.

Paying for his share of the damage made a hole in Winston's allowance, and added to the pressure on his already shaky finances. Income and expenditure never seemed to match and Mrs Everest wrote a worried letter telling Winston to be less profligate, and to reduce the financial

In 1891, Jennie, who decided that Winston was too grown up to need a nurse any more, decided to dismiss Mrs Everest. Winston and Jack became very upset and Winston protested vigorously at the prospect of losing his beloved 'Womanny'.

demands he made on his mother. But extravagance had long been a Marlborough family trait. Money problems continued to punctuate Winston's relations with Jennie – whom he looked on as his banker – for years to come.

At 17, Winston was able to fight harder than before against his parents' persistent failure to take his own wishes into account. A crisis came in December 1891 when Churchill refused to give up his Christmas holidays to live with a family in Rouen, France as a means of improving his French. He had declined to do so the previous year; this time, he put his case more forcefully.

In a three-page letter full of bitter recrimination, Winston told his mother: 'I am more unhappy than I can possibly say. Your unkindness has relieved me, however, from all feelings of duty.' When Jennie returned his letter after reading only one page because, she said, its style did not please her, Winston replied: 'I can perceive a reason for your not reading it .... I expect you were too busy with your parties and arrangements for Christmas. I comfort myself by this.'

PARENTAL NEGLECT

Throughout Winston's childhood, Jennie had often been too preoccupied with travelling, visiting or receiving friends, arranging and attending parties to have much time for her children. Both Winston and Jack were regularly sent to relatives for the holidays because they were in the way when the family home was full of guests at Christmas time or during the horseracing season, when London society did much of its entertaining. Lord Randolph paid

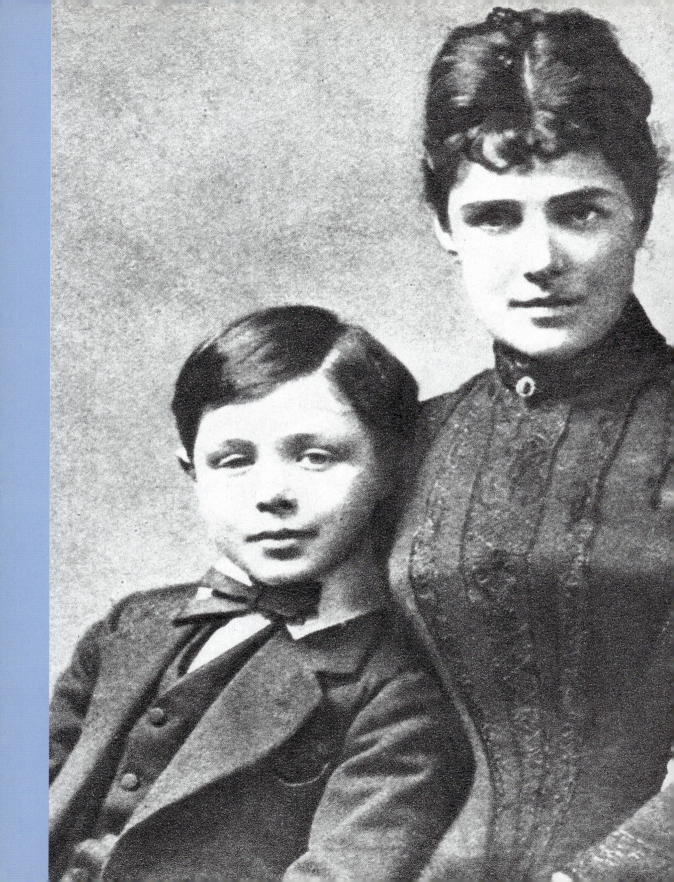

LADY RANDOLPH
CHURCHILL IN 1889, AT
THE AGE OF 35, WITH
HER SONS, WINSTON
AGED 15 AND JACK AGED
NINE. JENNIE WAS A
RENOWNED BEAUTY AND
GOSSIP HAD IT THAT SHE
TOOK MANY LOVERS.
ONE OF THEM, COLONEL
JOHN STRANGE JOCELYN,
5TH EARL OF RODEN,
WAS RUMOURED TO BE
JACK'S FATHER.

little more attention to his son than his wife did. In the spring of 1892, when Winston was preparing to compete in the Public Schools' Fencing Championships, he failed to persuade either of his parents to come to Aldershot to support him. Lord Randolph preferred to attend the Sandown horse races. Jennie went to Monte Carlo. Winston won the championship but the absence of his parents took the edge off his triumph.

That summer, Winston prepared to take the entrance examination for the Royal Military College at Sandhurst. He worked ten hours a day but to no avail. He failed, falling more than 1300 marks short of the standard required to enter the cavalry. Jennie, furious but not surprised, began to make plans to place Winston in a business firm. Among landowning aristocracy like the Marlboroughs, trade was a last resort. This unpalatable fate seemed to draw nearer for Winston when he retook the examination and failed again. It was little comfort that he had improved his position, falling only 351 marks below the passmark.

FEAR OF AN EARLY DEATH

In November 1892 a family tragedy occurred at Blenheim Palace; Winston's uncle, the eighth Duke of Marlborough, died suddenly at the age of 48. His son, Winston's first cousin and close friend Charles, known as 'Sunny', succeeded to the dukedom. Aged only 20 and as yet

unmarried, Sunny's accession opened up a tantalising prospect: Winston's father, Lord Randolph, became his nephew's heir, and until the new Duke had a son to succeed him, Winston was second in line.

Winston was more concerned by a disturbing pattern he had noticed in his family. Life, it seemed, was all too short for male Churchills.

Mrs Everest was the much-loved nurse who looked after both Winston and his younger brother Jack, pictured here. The boys adored Everest and at her death in 1895 they jointly provided the gravestone.

All boys at Harrow, including Winston, shown here in 1889, were required to wear the school's formal uniform of top hat and tails. Many other prominent leaders, including Robert Peel, Jawaharlal Nehru and Stanley Baldwin, were products of this prestigious public school.

James's crammer in London. The crammer force-fed students with information and the treatment, though drastic, worked. At long last, at his third attempt, late in July 1893, Winston passed the examination with 6309 marks – not quite enough to qualify for the infantry, but sufficient to place him fourth in the list of cavalry students. Winston was not only delighted and relieved, but thankful. 'If I had failed,' he told his mother, 'there would have been an end of all my chances. As it is, my fate is in my own hands and I have a fresh start.'

Many years before, three of Lord Randolph's brothers had died in infancy, and now a fourth was gone in his forties. Winston's own brother Jack had at first been pronounced stillborn and he was himself constantly plagued by illness. This dismal record convinced Churchill that he would, in his turn, die young and be denied the destiny which he was increasingly certain lay before him. This fear would plague him for many years. In 1914, when he reached his 40th birthday, he remarked: 'Is it 40 and finished?'

Twenty years earlier, Winston was already impatient to make his mark before it was too late. Qualifying for Sandhurst became an urgent necessity and the first half of 1893 was almost entirely occupied with intensive work at Captain

CHURCHILL ON HIS SCHOOL DAYS

I was on the whole considerably discouraged by my school days. Except in fencing, in which I had won the Public School Championship, I had achieved no distinction. All my contemporaries and even younger boys seemed in every way better adapted to the conditions of our little world. They were far better both at the games and the lessons. It is not pleasant to feel oneself so completely outclassed and left behind at the very beginning of the race.

WINSTON GOES TO WAR

After graduating from Sandhurst in 1895, Churchill saw action in wars in Cuba, India, the Sudan and South Africa. These campaigns also provided him with material for his first writings, but the Boer war in South Africa offered something extra: taken prisoner, Churchill escaped, hit the headlines and became a popular celebrity.

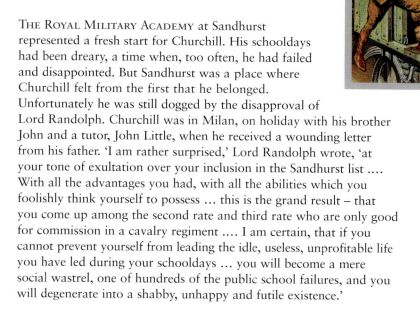

The Royal Military Academy at Sandhurst represented a fresh start for Churchill. His schooldays had been dreary, a time when, too often, he had failed and disappointed. But Sandhurst was a place where Churchill felt from the first that he belonged. Unfortunately he was still dogged by the disapproval of Lord Randolph. Churchill was in Milan, on holiday with his brother John and a tutor, John Little, when he received a wounding letter from his father. 'I am rather surprised,' Lord Randolph wrote, 'at your tone of exultation over your inclusion in the Sandhurst list .... With all the advantages you had, with all the abilities which you foolishly think yourself to possess ... this is the grand result – that you come up among the second rate and third rate who are only good for commission in a cavalry regiment .... I am certain, that if you cannot prevent yourself from leading the idle, useless, unprofitable life you have led during your schooldays ... you will become a mere social wastrel, one of hundreds of the public school failures, and you will degenerate into a shabby, unhappy and futile existence.'

As a young cadet at Sandhurst in 1894, Churchill (far left) enjoyed a '... time of high hopes and good friends', as he later wrote.
Churchill's daring escape from a Boer prisoner of war camp in 1899 (above) brought him fame. He concealed himself on a train bound for Portuguese East Africa.

In 1895, Churchill gained his first experience of army life with the 4th Hussars. The Hussars were a light cavalry regiment who wore uniforms inspired by the elaborate dress uniform of 15th-century Hungarian light horsemen.

Churchill was deeply depressed by this damning indictment. When he returned to England in September, he was astonished to learn that his father had used his influence to obtain a place for him in an infantry regiment, the 60th Rifles. But Colonel John Brabazon, commander of a cavalry regiment, the 4th Queen's Own Hussars, already had his eye on Churchill. Despite his father's disapproval, Churchill was unable to resist Brabazon's invitation to become a Hussar officer.

Lord Randolph was becoming increasingly capricious in his behaviour. He was, at this stage, already dying, probably from tertiary syphilis, a disease that progressively destroys the nervous system and severely damages the brain. But Churchill was unaware of the serious nature of his father's malady.

ROMANCE AND TRAGEDY

Sandhurst took Churchill's mind off his father's unpredictable moods. Military training kept him busy, with parades and drills. It was a strenuous life and had its perils. Churchill 'scraped his tail', as his mother put it, in a riding accident, and almost collapsed with fatigue after a half-kilometre (550-yard) run carrying full kit and rifle.

A certain Miss Polly Hacket, whom Churchill met in London, occupied much of his attention in the first half of 1894. He took Polly for a walk down fashionable Bond Street and bought her some sweets. But the romance did not prosper and a year later Polly married someone else.

While Churchill was still paying court to Polly Hacket, his father's condition worsened. In the House of Commons, he slurred his words while

CHURCHILL ON HORSES

Horses were the greatest of my pleasures at Sandhurst. I and the group in which I moved spent all our money on hiring horses from the very excellent local livery stables ... we organised point to points and even a steeplechase in the park of a friendly grandee, and bucketed gaily about the countryside .... No one ever came to grief ... by riding horses. No hour of life is lost that is spent in the saddle. Young men have often been ruined through owning horses, or through backing horses, but never through riding them; unless of course they break their necks which, taken at a gallop, is a very good death to die.

making speeches and often forgot what he meant to say. In June 1894, Jennie took her ailing husband on a world tour, perhaps as a means of preventing his deterioration from becoming too public. But by November, he was suffering delusions and was unable to speak. Jennie had no option but to cut short the tour and bring him home. Lord Randolph died early on 24 January, 1895. He was buried three days later at Bladon, just outside the walls of Blenheim Palace.

A HUNGER FOR ACTION

Shortly before his father's death, Churchill passed his examinations at Sandhurst, coming 20th in a class of 130. On 20 February, he was gazetted second lieutenant in the 4th Hussars, a prominent light cavalry regiment stationed at Aldershot. The routine at Aldershot was pleasant and leisurely. There was 'breakfast in bed' at 7:45AM, two hours of riding in the morning and drill in the afternoon, followed by hot baths and evenings spent playing billiards and cards. Manoeuvres, which could involve spending eight hours in the saddle followed by another two tending the horses in the stables, used up plenty of energy, as did polo, a game Churchill played with enthusiasm.

But self-imposed study, however absorbing, was not enough to content a young man of ambition. Winston Churchill craved action and the thrill of being at the centre of important events as they unfolded. In 1895, the stage that provided Churchill with the drama he wanted was a long way off. In Cuba, the Spanish who had ruled the Caribbean island for more than 500 years were now struggling to contain rebels who were waging a violent battle for independence. This

On campaign, Churchill wore the khaki uniform adopted by the British Army in the late 19th century. The new khaki uniforms helped to camouflage the soldiers unlike the red uniforms previously worn, which had marked them out as targets for enemy snipers.

CHURCHILL AFTER PASSING OUT AT SANDHURST

I passed out of Sandhurst into the world. It opened like Aladdin's cave. From the beginning of 1895 down to the present time of writing (1930), I have never had time to turn round. I could count almost on my fingers the days when I have had nothing to do. An endless moving picture in which one was an actor. On the whole, great fun! But the years 1895 to 1900 ... exceed in vividness, variety and exertion anything I have known. When I look back upon them I cannot but return my sincere thanks to the high gods for the gift of existence ....

was exactly the sort of scenario that appealed to Churchill, but the Cuban war of independence was not simply a chance for adventure.

Life in the 4th Hussars was expensive and Churchill's army salary of about £65 a month provided less than one third of the sum required to fund the lifestyle of a cavalry officer. His mother's contributions were limited by her own extravagance. The answer to Churchill's financial problems was journalism. He persuaded a British newspaper, the *Daily Graphic*, to pay for eyewitness reports from the front in Cuba. As a serving officer, Churchill also needed to justify his Cuban venture to the army so he agreed to provide intelligence and statistics, and to report on the performance of a new bullet being used in the war for the first time.

With a friend, Reginald Barnes, Churchill set sail for Cuba on board the Cunard Royal Mail steamship *Etruria* at the end of October 1895. He arrived on the island three weeks later. Churchill's five reports from Cuba were published in Britain as *Letters from the Front* by W S C. The fighting not only gave the young reporter a taste of life under fire but enabled him to witness how much hardship and sacrifice the Cubans were willing to undergo to achieve their freedom. Churchill came to believe that, despite using the methods of 'incendiarists and brigands', the Cubans' struggle

for independence was justified, chiefly because of the widespread corruption in the ruling Spanish government and the punitive taxes demanded of the poverty-stricken Cubans. This was an unusually liberal stance for someone of his background and class, but he disliked being pigeon-holed and hated mindless conformity. These independent tendencies would one day vex Churchill's political allies as much as his opponents, and cause furore in Parliament.

After three weeks in Cuba, Churchill returned to England with plentiful supplies of Havana cigars – a lifelong preference – Cuban coffee and a great delicacy, guava jelly. Unfortunately, he returned to a widely publicised scandal. While at Aldershot, Churchill was involved in efforts to make an unpopular officer-cadet, Alan Bruce, resign from the 4th Hussars. Bruce left the regiment, but his father, A C Bruce-Pryce, determined on revenge and charged Churchill with 'acts of gross immorality' allegedly committed at Sandhurst. Churchill took the case to the High Court, where the judge found the charge spurious. Bruce's father withdrew the allegation and paid £400 damages. But the so-called 'cavalry scandal' took a long time to die down.

After the thrills and dangers of the fighting in Cuba, Churchill longed to find another battlefield. The 4th Hussars were due to sail for service in India but Churchill feared this would place him even further away from the most lively scenes of action. Wars against rebel forces were pending in Egypt, Cyprus and in Matabeleland in South Africa. Churchill begged his mother to use her influence with her friend, Lord Lansdowne, the Secretary of State for War, but he warned Jennie that it might look bad if her son left Britain while the press was still headlining his alleged misdemeanours at Sandhurst.

Churchill saw action for the first time on 16 September, 1897 when he fought with the Malakand Field Force, defending India's disputed northwest frontier against a force of ferocious Afghan and Afridi tribesmen.

BOREDOM IN INDIA

Frustrated and disappointed, Churchill sailed for India with the 4th Hussars on 11 September, 1896. Arriving in October, the regiment was stationed in Bangalore in the hills west of Madras, which had a cool and pleasant climate. In Bangalore Churchill shared a pink and white stucco palace with two other officers, Reginald Barnes, his companion in Cuba, and Hugo Baring. Its most spectacular feature was a rose garden full of splendidly coloured butterflies.

Life in Bangalore was relaxed – breakfast at 5:00AM, parade at 6:00AM, followed by another breakfast, a bath and a little paperwork, but then little more to do between 8:00AM and 4:15PM, when the polo playing began. It was an idle life, which Churchill regarded as a waste of time. To him, British India, full of obsequious natives and petty administrators on the make, was a 'godless land of snobs and bores'. Calcutta, which Churchill visited late in 1896, was 'full of supremely uninteresting people'.

> To Churchill, British India was a 'godless land of snobs and bores'. Calcutta, which Churchill visited late in 1896, was 'full of supremely uninteresting people'.

His thoughts turned more and more to a career in politics and he viewed every experience and achievement as preparation for it. He believed, for instance, that as a Brigade Major, a rank he achieved early in 1897, his chances of winning a seat in Parliament would be enhanced. But his liberal political views – particularly his support for the Greek insurgents on the island of Crete, who were in revolt against their Turkish rulers – created 'pious horror' among his fellow officers.

A CALL TO ARMS

When the Turks declared war Churchill resolved to claim a piece of the action, and some useful fees as a war reporter. He took a month's leave

Churchill enjoyed a luxurious lifestyle while he was serving with the 4th Queen's Own Hussars in India. 'Princes could live no better than we,' he wrote.

Sir Bindon Blood, commander of the Malakand Field Force in 1897, was a direct descendant of Colonel Blood, who in the reign of King Charles II attempted to steal the Crown jewels from the Tower of London.

and left for Europe. By the time his ship reached Italy, the Turks had defeated the Greek forces and the fighting was over. A disappointed Churchill returned to Britain, where he made his first political speech at a meeting of the Primrose League near Bath on 26 June. His father had co-founded the League in 1883 to popularise Tory ideas. As his first theme, he spoke of Tory Democracy, a liberal version of Conservatism, praised recent government moves to pay compensation to workmen injured in dangerous trades, and expressed the hope that the labourer would one day become 'a shareholder in the business in which he worked'. This was radical talk and it shocked his audiences.

Back in Bangalore three weeks later, Churchill began writing a novel, *Savrola*, a romance with a political slant set in an imaginary republic. Churchill was just warming to his plot when he received a letter from Sir Bindon Blood, commander of a Field Force recently formed to quash a revolt among Pathan tribesmen on the northwest frontier of India. Churchill had met Sir Bindon at the house of his

CHURCHILL ON TRAINING WITH THE 4TH HUSSARS

I am all for youth being made willingly to endure austerities; and for the rest, it was a gay and lordly life .... The young officers were often permitted to ride out with their troops at exercise or on route marches .... There is a thrill and charm of its own in the glittering jingle of a cavalry squadron manoeuvring at the trot; and this deepens into joyous excitement when the same evolutions are performed at a gallop. The stir of the horses, the clank of their equipment, the thrill of motion, the tossing plumes, the sense of incorporation in a living machine, the suave dignity of the uniform – all combined to make cavalry drill a fine thing in itself.

In 1896 the British Army fortified the ruins of this old Moghul fort (left), close to the Malakand Pass between British-ruled India and Afghanistan where Churchill fought in 1897. It is now known as Churchill's Picket. Having resigned from the army, Churchill (right) went to South Africa in 1899 as war correspondent for the Daily Mail *and* Morning Post. *Churchill had no illusions about war: 'however sure you are that you can easily win ... there would not be a war if the other man did not think he also had a chance.'*

aunt, Duchess Lily, on his recent visit to Britain. Sir Bindon had promised to include Churchill in any frontier campaign he might lead in future, and now, in August 1897, his chance for action finally arrived.

FRONTIER CAMPAIGN

Elated, Churchill left Bangalore for the frontier, more than 2175 miles away, on 29 August. His mother had already persuaded the *Daily Telegraph* to print his reports, and Churchill himself arranged to send a daily telegram from the front to the *Allahabad Pioneer* in India. This was Churchill's greatest journalistic coup so far, but as always, his

political prospects were uppermost in his mind. He wrote to his mother: 'I feel that the fact of having seen service with British troops while still a young man must give me more weight politically ... and may perhaps improve my prospects of gaining popularity with the country.'

In early September Churchill reached Malakand on the northwest frontier. This mountainous region was British-Indian territory but the Afghan and Afridi tribesmen who lived along the border were fiercely independent and deeply resented British attempts to control their lives. These ferocious warriors, who were known to cut to pieces any wounded left on the battlefield, were engaged in

CHURCHILL ON THE PUBLICATION OF HIS FIRST BOOK

The Malakand Field Force has an immediate and wide success. The reviewers ... vied with each other in praise. When the first bundle of reviews reached me together with the volume as published, I was filled with pride and pleasure at the compliments .... Remember I had never been praised before. The only comments which had ever been made upon my work at school had been 'Indifferent', 'Untidy', 'Slovenly', 'Bad', 'Very bad' etc. Now here was the great world with its leading literary newspaper and vigilant erudite critics, writing whole columns of praise!

violent, bloody warfare against the British Army forces, which included regiments of Indian sepoys, such as the Punjab Irregulars. When Churchill arrived in 1896 to take part in the Malakand Campaign, some 50,000 of these British and Indian troops faced the tribesmen from across the border.

The dangers did not inhibit Churchill's reckless bravery. Ordered by General Blood to join the second brigade of the Malakand Field Force, Churchill put himself in the thick of the fighting. He took up a dangerously exposed position within range of Afridi rifle fire and when the British troops withdrew, he was the last to leave the scene. In the confusion Churchill fired at almost point blank range to kill an Afridi who was about to slice up a wounded British officer, and afterwards rescued a wounded Sikh from the same fate.

Churchill remained in action with the Malakand Field Force for the next month. He spent hours under fire and was often involved in bloody close-quarter fighting. When the fighting was over he emerged unscathed, though shocked by the barbarities he had witnessed on both sides. The Afridis, he wrote, 'kill and mutilate everyone they catch and we do not hesitate to finish their wounded off.'

The horrors he witnessed quickly faded from Churchill's mind. Back in Bangalore in the third week of October, he wrote that his time on the northwest frontier had been 'the most glorious and delightful that my life has yet contained'. He was pleased to receive a campaign medal and, for his prowess, a mention in dispatches.

'I am more ambitious for a reputation for personal courage,' he wrote to his mother, 'than anything else in the world … I feel I took every chance and displayed myself with ostentation wherever there was danger.' Malakand, Churchill concluded, 'was quite a foundation for political life'.

PUBLISHED AUTHOR

Churchill's first published book, *The Story of the Malakand Field Force: An Episode of Frontier War*, appeared in London in March 1898 and was reprinted the following year. It was a success

and marked Churchill out as a promising young writer. The book also provided a solution to the pressing problem of his finances, which had been rapidly depleted by Jennie's extravagant spending. The problem was so dire that, by 1898, only three years after her husband's death, Churchill had to warn his mother that her spending on clothes, entertaining and travel had cost one quarter of 'our entire fortune in the world'. But the Malakand campaign proved to be a lucrative experience for Churchill: he earned

around £400 from his book and his newspaper reports, representing some £20,000 or more in today's money.

Churchill's writing did little for his popularity in the 4th Hussars. His fellow officers resented his opportunism and his profits. In the military and aristocratic ethos of the time, Churchill's interest in self-promotion, medal-hunting and moneymaking was considered vulgar. Churchill had also acquired a reputation for bumptiousness that irritated his mother,

On board the liner Dunottar Castle, *Churchill (second row, second from the left) joined other correspondents heading for South Africa to report on the Boer War.*

among many others. In a letter to Jennie, for example, Churchill boasted about how he managed to escape death at Malakand. 'I am so conceited,' he wrote, 'I do not believe the gods would create so potent a being as myself for so prosaic an ending.'

Churchill, seen here in the uniform of the South African Light Horse, had his hatred of war reinforced by the fighting against the Boers. Just visible is the thin moustache which featured in his description after he escaped from a Boer prison camp.

DESERT SHOWDOWN

Churchill was still thirsting for the heat of battle when he had a stroke of good luck. He was on leave in England in July 1898 when the Prime Minister, Lord Salisbury, who had been impressed by his book, invited him to 10 Downing Street. Salisbury arranged for Churchill to transfer to the 21st Lancers, who were due to leave for the Sudan under the command of General Herbert Kitchener.

A showdown was imminent between the Anglo-Egyptian forces and the Dervishes, led by the Muslim holy man, the Mahdi, who had conquered the Egyptian-ruled Sudan 14 years earlier. The Egyptians wanted their territory back and the British had their own grievances: they wanted to avenge the death of General Charles Gordon, murdered by Dervishes at Khartoum in 1885. The Dervishes had resisted all attempts to regain control over the Sudan, but in September 1898, Kitchener was at last in a position to bring them to battle with a good chance of victory. The battleground was the fortress of Omdurman, which lay on the Nile north of Khartoum.

The Anglo-Egyptian army of 26,000 men faced a force of 40,000 Dervishes but superiority in numbers counted for little in the face of Kitchener's mechanised weaponry. The wave of Dervishes which swept towards the British positions, yelling ferocious war cries, were felled by the hundreds in a blaze of machine gun and small arms fire. In his autobiography *My Early Life*, Churchill described the scene: 'After an enormous carnage, exceeding 20,000 men who strewed the ground in heaps and swathes like snowdrifts, the whole mass of the Dervishes dissolved into fragments and into particles and streamed away into the fantastic mirages of the desert.'

Anxious that the Dervishes might retreat and take the city of Khartoum, 3 miles from Omdurman, Kitchener ordered the 21st Lancers, Churchill's cavalry regiment, to sweep the field of Dervishes before they could regroup. But this was no easy task. Churchill was in command of a group of around 25 men. 'I was riding a handy, sure-footed grey Arab polo pony,' he wrote, ' … I

'Horses spouting blood, struggling on three legs. Men bleeding from terrible wounds, … arms and faces cut to pieces, bowels protruding, men gasping, crying, collapsing, expiring.'

CHURCHILL ON THE ARTILLERY BARRAGE AGAINST THE DERVISHES ADVANCING AT OMDURMAN

The cannonade turned upon them. Two or three batteries and all the gunboats, at least thirty guns, opened an intense fire. Their shells … burst in scores over the heads and among the masses …. Down went their standards by dozens and their men by hundreds. Wide gaps and shapeless heaps appeared in their array. One saw them jumping and tumbling under the shrapnel bursts; but none turned back.

Churchill (in front of the group, wearing a forage cap) was held captive by the Boers in a teacher-training college in Pretoria which had been converted into a prisoner-of-war camp. He hated his time in captivity, which reminded him of his schooldays.

saw immediately before me, and now only half a length of a polo ground away, the row of crouching blue figures [Dervishes] firing frantically, wreathed in white smoke .... We were going at a fast but steady gallop .... I looked again towards the enemy. The scene appeared to be suddenly transformed. The blue-black men were still firing, but behind them there now came into view a depression like a shallow, sunken road. This was crowded and crammed with men rising up from the ground where they had hidden .... The Dervishes appeared to be ten or twelve deep at the thickest, a great grey mass gleaming with steel.' Churchill's men increased their speed to the fastest gallop. 'The collision was now very near,' he continued. 'I saw immediately before me ... the two blue men who lay in my path. They were perhaps a couple of yards apart. I rode at the interval between them. They both fired. I passed through the smoke, conscious that I was unhurt ... The trooper immediately behind me was killed.'

A few moments later, another Dervish, this time armed with a spear, suddenly jumped up and made for Churchill, weapon raised to strike. Churchill shot him dead when he was less than three yards away. The first charge over, Churchill expected an order to charge again, but there was no need. The Dervishes were retreating and the battle was over. Omdurman cost some 500 Anglo-Egyptian casualties and 25,000 Dervishes were killed or injured.

The scene after the battle was appalling. 'Horses spouting blood, struggling on three legs,' Churchill recorded later, 'Men bleeding from terrible wounds, fish-hook spears stuck right through them, arms and faces cut to pieces, bowels protruding, men gasping, crying, collapsing, expiring.'

The experience convinced Churchill that war was an abberation in the life of a civilised nation, and an occasion for letting loose barbarities that were not the monopoly of native tribesmen like the Afridis or Dervishes. As Churchill revealed in his 1899 book on the Sudan campaign, *The River War*, atrocities were also committed on the British side – including the killing of thousands of wounded Dervishes and the desecration of the tomb and corpse of the Mahdi, the former holy leader of the Dervishes. In military circles, Churchill was heavily criticised for these embarrassing revelations and particularly for charging General Kitchener with responsibility. In spite of, or

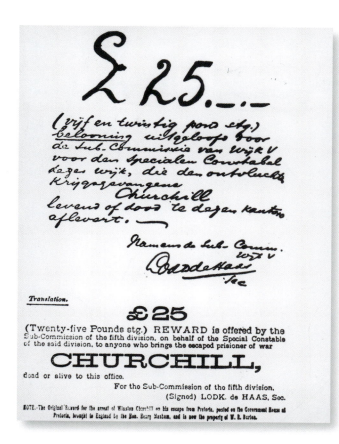

The Boers posted a £25 reward for Churchill, dead or alive. During his three days hiding in a mine, Churchill smoked a cigar. An African boy smelled the smoke, saw a white man in the mine and bolted, convinced he had seen a ghost.

perhaps because of, its controversial stance, *The River War* was a considerable success.

By the time *The River War* was published, Churchill had resigned from the army. After Omdurman, he briefly returned to Bangalore and the 4th Hussars, remained there long enough to help the regiment win a polo competition, and in the third week of March 1899 departed, never to see India again.

TO CAPE TOWN

Churchill felt well placed for the next step in his life and career. He had proved himself a hero on the battlefield and had attracted publicity with his writings. He was now ready to enter politics. But the electorate at Oldham, where he stood as candidate in a by-election in July 1899, had other ideas. Churchill campaigned hard, but lost.

Despite this setback, he was not at a loose end for long. Another colonial war was brewing,

this time in South Africa where a long-standing dispute between Britain and the Boer Republic of the Transvaal had come to a head in the autumn of 1899. Rumours were circulating that British workers in the Witwatersrand goldfield were being ill-treated, but the real cause of the war was possession of the lucrative region. On 18 September the *Daily Mail* asked Churchill to go to South Africa as their correspondent. Churchill accepted, but doubled his prospects by also offering to report for the *Morning Post* for a £1000 fee with all expenses paid.

When Churchill arrived at Cape Town on 31 October, 1899, he faced the greatest adventure of his life. The South African War was a struggle between the unwieldy British Army and a force of nimble, skilful guerrillas. Before the British could get to grips with this unfamiliar mode of warfare, the Boers scored a series of victories, invading Natal and laying siege to Mafeking, Kimberley and Ladysmith.

CHURCHILL ON THE SOUTH AFRICAN WAR

Ah, horrible war, amazing medley of the glorious and the squalid, the pitiful and the sublime .... Much as war attracts me and fascinates my mind with its tremendous situations, I feel more deeply every year and can measure the feeling here in the midst of arms, what vile and wicked folly and barbarism it is.

CAPTURED

On 15 November, 1899, a short way down the rail line from Ladysmith, Churchill boarded an armoured train with 150 other men. The train drove on for two stations before a party of 50 Boers was spotted dangerously close to the line.

A few minutes later, the train ran into an ambush and the Boers opened fire. One shell hit the leading truck. The train then ran into a stone on the line, which derailed three of the trucks.

Six weeks after the train ambush in which he was captured, Churchill returned to his former prison with soldiers sent to release British troops held there by the Boers. One of the prisoners, Melville Goodacre, recorded in his diary: 'Suddenly, Winston Churchill came galloping over the hill and tore down the Boer flag and hoisted ours, amid cheers.'

Churchill bravely attempted to unhitch the intact trucks to allow the train to run back along the line to safety, but failed. About 500 armed Boers were ranged along the embankment; Churchill and his companions were forced to surrender.

The prisoners were marched to a prisoner-of-war camp in the Model School in Pretoria, capital of the Transvaal, where Churchill at once began to plan his escape. He made his first attempt on 11 December, but was thwarted by the vigilance of the Boer guards. The following night Churchill was successful. He climbed the wall next to a latrine and dropped down in the darkness of the garden on the other side. Two other would-be escapees, Captain Aylmer Haldane and Sergeant-Major Brockie, were unable to follow him and Churchill went on alone.

Safety lay about 275 miles away at the port of Lourenço Marques in Portuguese East Africa.

Somewhat dishevelled, Churchill found an excited, vociferous crowd awaiting him at Durban when he arrived there after his escape from prison. 'After an hour of turmoil,' he wrote, 'which I frankly admit I enjoyed extremely, I escaped to the train.'

Churchill headed for the railway line which, he knew, ran to the port from Pretoria. He did not have long to wait before a train arrived. Just as it was slowing down to enter a station, he jumped in a wagon full of empty coal sacks. When daylight came, Churchill left the train for fear of being seen, and spent the day hiding by the track at Witbank. By this time, he was a marked man. His escape had been discovered, and his photograph and description were being circulated across the Transvaal: 'Englishman, 25 years old … average build, walks with a slight stoop, pale appearance, red brown hair, almost invisible small moustache, speaks through the nose … cannot speak Dutch, last seen in a brown suit of clothes.' The Boers even mentioned Churchill's inability to pronounce the letter 's'.

ON THE RUN

After two nights on the run, Churchill was so hungry, thirsty and desperate that he took a big risk. He headed for some lights he had seen a short way off, and found they lit up a coal mine. He knocked on the door of a nearby house. The man who answered pointed a pistol at him, fearful that his caller might be a Boer spy. But Churchill's risk paid off. The man was John Howard, manager of the coal mine and an Englishman.

For three days, Howard hid Churchill in the mine, with rats for company. Eventually, on the evening of 19 December, after a week on the run, Churchill was smuggled onto a railway wagon. Hidden under bales of wool, he continued his journey to Portuguese East Africa. Just short of the border the train was shunted into a siding, where it remained for 18 hours. Fortunately, Howard had supplied Churchill with food and drink – two roast chickens, some cold meat, bread, a melon and three bottles of cold tea.

The Boers searched Churchill's wagon while it lay in the siding, but they missed him. At last, the train started moving towards the border. The signal that he had successfully eluded the Boers was the first station with a Portuguese name. When he saw it, Churchill jumped up out of the wool bales, black with coal from head to foot, shouting at the top of his voice. For good measure, he fired his revolver two or three times in the air.

Churchill lost no time letting the press know that he was free. On 21 December, he sent a long telegram from Lourenço Marques to the *Morning Post* entitled 'How I Escaped from Pretoria'. Within days, his exploit had made him famous in Britain and throughout the Empire. When he arrived by ship at Durban, in South Africa, two days before Christmas 1899, enthusiastic crowds crammed the quayside to cheer him. At last, Winston Leonard Spencer Churchill was the celebrity he had longed to be.

CHURCHILL BECAME AN
INSTANT CELEBRITY
AFTER HIS ESCAPE FROM
THE BOERS AND WAS
GIVEN A HERO'S
WELCOME WHEN HE
ARRIVED IN DURBAN.
HIS EXPLOIT PROVED AN
IMPORTANT BOOST TO
FLAGGING MORALE, FOR
THE BRITISH ARMY HAD
RECENTLY SUFFERED TWO
MAJOR DEFEATS, AT
MAGERSFONTEIN, CAPE
COLONY ON 11
DECEMBER, 1899 AND AT
COLENSO IN NATAL
FOUR DAYS LATER.

WINSTON THE POLITICIAN

IN 1900, CHURCHILL WAS ELECTED TO PARLIAMENT, BUT HIS 'SOCIALISTIC' IDEAS ABOUT WELFARE WERE UNPOPULAR WITH HIS FELLOW CONSERVATIVES. MANY NEVER FORGAVE HIM FOR 'CROSSING THE FLOOR' TO JOIN THE LIBERALS IN 1904. CHURCHILL SOON ROSE TO HIGH POSITION. BY 1908, THE YEAR HE MARRIED, HE WAS A GOVERNMENT MINISTER AND MEMBER OF THE CABINET.

CHURCHILL'S ESCAPE FROM CAPTIVITY was a welcome distraction from the dismal news of the reverses the British suffered in the first months of the war in South Africa. His arrival in Durban was greeted with frenzied excitement. The crowd carried him shoulder high to the Town Hall, where he gave an impromptu speech describing his adventures. Later, Churchill confessed that he had enjoyed every moment of it.

He had not yet finished with the war in South Africa and in January 1900 he accepted an offer from General Sir Redvers Buller to enlist as a lieutenant in the South African Light Horse. He departed for Ladysmith, which was still under siege.

A recent War Office order had banned serving officers from doubling as war reporters, following Churchill's exploits in the Sudan. But Churchill agreed to serve without pay to preserve his status as a correspondent for the *Morning Post*. He was not unduly worried about soldiering unpaid. For once, money was not a major problem.

Election campaigns, such as this one (left) in Manchester in April 1908, were ideal settings for Churchill to display his skills as an orator. He had a theatrical way with words and a knack for creating memorable phrases.
Churchill became an MP (above) in 1901. It was the start of a parliamentary career that would span the next 64 years.

His name as a newspaper correspondent was made; journalism earned him 12 times the army salary for his rank. He had finished his novel *Savrola*, which was due for publication in 1900, and his book on the South African War, *London to Ladysmith via Pretoria*, would appear the same year.

Churchill was conscious that Britain had unfinished business in the war and national pride to restore, and continued to serve in South Africa until it was clear that the British Army was gaining the upper hand. He was present when the siege of Ladysmith was lifted at the end of February 1900, and three months later took part in the British invasion of the Transvaal which finally put paid to the series of Boer victories.

A LIBERAL IN DISGUISE

Churchill's service in South Africa came to an end on 7 July, 1900, when he left Cape Town for home. His new life in politics, so long awaited and so carefully planned, was about to begin. The Conservative constituents of Oldham, where Churchill had failed to win a seat in the by-election the year before, invited him to stand again. The 'Khaki Election', so called because of the influence the Boer war cast over it, was held

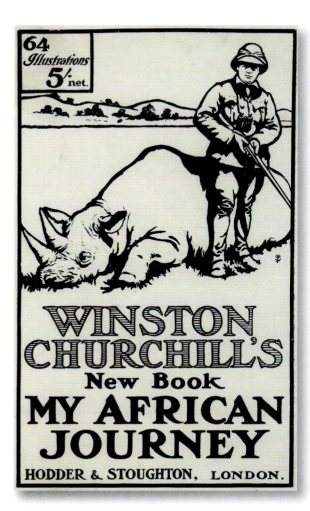

The material for My African Journey, *published in 1908, came from a series of articles Churchill wrote for* Strand *magazine during a five-month journey through Kenya, Uganda, the Sudan and along the Nile in 1907.*

CHURCHILL ON HIS RETURN TO BRITAIN IN 1900

I received the warmest of welcomes on returning home. Oldham almost without distinction of party accorded me a triumph. I entered the town in state in a procession of ten landaus and drove through streets crowded with enthusiastic operatives and mill girls. I described my escape (from prison) to a tremendous meeting in the Theatre Royal. When I mentioned the name of Mr. Dewsnap, the Oldham engineer who had wound me down the mine, the audience shouted: 'His wife's in the gallery'. There was general jubilation.

in October. Churchill won one of the two seats being contested in Oldham, and on 14 February, 1901 he took his seat in the House of Commons.

On 18 February, Churchill made his maiden speech in Parliament, which was described by the *Daily Express* newspaper as 'spell binding'. The popular magazine *Punch* was so impressed that its regular parliamentary report was entirely devoted to Churchill's performance. Throughout his career, the news that Winston Churchill was on his feet and about to speak rapidly filled the benches in the Commons, no matter what the subject.

Fighting in South Africa ceased in May 1902. Churchill was anxious that the defeated Boers should be treated generously, and was relieved that the terms of the peace treaty were lenient, even including £3 million of compensation for farms destroyed in the fighting. All his life, Churchill would appreciate guerrilla fighters who, like the Boers, fearlessly pitted themselves against the ruling powers.

A pro-Boer stance was not popular with the electorate. It was one of the reasons why the Liberals, who advertised themselves as an anti-war party, lost the 'Khaki Election' of 1900. Although not anti-war, Churchill was in many ways a Liberal in Conservative clothing. His political philosophy, like his father's, was Tory Democracy, which promoted the social duties he felt Conservative governments ought to perform. Churchill passionately believed in policies advocating a reasonable standard of living for all, the good health and welfare of the working class, unemployment benefits and pensions.

Only a year after he first entered Parliament, Churchill had already attracted the attention of political cartoonists. They regarded his babyish face and rotund form as a gift to their art, but as his political career progressed, Churchill's gritty determination and wartime defiance of Hitler frequently saw him depicted as the stubborn British Bulldog.

LECTURE TOUR

Outside Parliament, good speakers could command £265 for a single lecture. Shortly after he was elected as MP for Oldham, Churchill engaged a professional agent. Churchill was a natural for the life of a touring lecturer: young and energetic, still basking in the celebrity he had earned in South Africa and able to deliver thrilling first-hand accounts of battles in faraway places. He attracted large audiences and could hold their attention for 90 minutes or more.

It was hard work. In October and November 1900, Churchill delivered 30 lectures in seven weeks in cities as far apart as Dundee in Scotland and Belfast and Dublin in Ireland. Then he toured abroad, giving lectures across the United States and Canada, some of which earned him up to $1000 a time. Meanwhile he continued to address, and at times harangue, his fellow MPs in Parliament. Even at this early stage, his speeches revealed the taste for controversy that would characterise so much of Churchill's parliamentary career. In May 1901, only three months after entering Parliament, Churchill attacked his own side, the Conservative government of Lord Salisbury, on an important matter of policy. He condemned the 15 per cent increase in army expenditure proposed by St John Brodrick, the Secretary of State for War.

Churchill told the House of Commons on 13 May: 'We must avoid a servile imitation of the clanking military empires of the Europe continent,

by which we cannot obtain the military predominance and security which is desired.' For an ex-army man this was a surprising, even shocking, attitude, but a glance at a map of Europe showed that there was sound reasoning behind it. If danger ever threatened an island country like Britain, Churchill warned, it would come from the sea, not the land. St John Brodrick's 15 per cent increase would be much better spent on building up the Royal Navy, so underlining its established mastery of the seas. He went on to suggest a higher, moral reason for not increasing the size of the military.

'It is known alike by peoples and by rulers,' Churchill went on, citing the benefits the British empire had brought to the world of his day, 'that on the whole British influence is healthy and kindly, and makes for the general happiness and welfare of mankind. And we shall make a fatal bargain if we allow the moral force which this country has so long exerted to become diminished, or perhaps even destroyed for the sake of the costly, trumpery, dangerous military playthings on which the Secretary of State for War has set his heart.'

> 'We shall make a fatal bargain if we allow the moral force which this country has so long exerted to become diminished, or perhaps even destroyed for the sake of the ... military playthings on which the Secretary of State for War has set his heart.'

As a war correspondent in South Africa, where he sat for this sketch, Churchill had realised that his non-combatant status was no guarantee of his safety. He wrote of his position after his capture by the Boers in 1899: 'I had enough military law to know that a civilian in a half uniform who has taken an active and prominent part in a fight, even if he has not fired a shot himself, is liable to be shot at once by a drumhead court martial.'

REBEL MP

The government was dismayed that one of their own MPs should turn against them in this way, all the more because the Liberal and Radical opposition was so delighted. Churchill soon became associated with a group of renegade young Conservatives who, like him, were dissatisfied with many aspects of government policy. They were known as the 'Hooligans' or 'Hughligans', after one of their members, Lord Hugh Cecil, who was the son of the Prime Minister, Lord Salisbury, although he did not support his policies.

Churchill was more than merely dissatisfied with mainstream Conservatism. Politically, he was out of sympathy with it. Always radical in his thinking, he was fast moving towards the Liberal Party. Their aims, like Churchill's, gave high priority to social policies: healthcare, better housing and education, and secure employment for the working classes.

By 1902, Churchill was waging almost unremitting political warfare, both in and out of Parliament. He lashed the Conservatives for neglecting the plight of the poor and targeted MPs who favoured a protectionist policy known as Imperial Preference. The policy advocated the creation of tariffs on foreign imports as a means of preserving the market for goods coming in from territories of the British empire. This had the effect of raising the price of food and so hit poor families hardest. Instead, he advocated free trade and no tariffs. Inevitably, he drew fierce Conservative fire for his disloyalty, and for his disruptive influence in the House of Commons.

Despite the vigour of his attacks, it was far from easy for Churchill to split with the party his

father had supported for 20 years. Instead, he tried a middle way – a free food league within the Conservative Party, which could put the free trade case in Parliament. When the league was launched in July 1902, under the name of Unionist Free Traders, 60 Conservative MPs joined. But they soon felt uncomfortable with Churchill's vociferous attacks on government ministers. In addition, his open support for a Liberal candidate in a coming by-election smacked of betrayal.

Churchill was shunned by the Conservative Party, both in and out of Parliament, and in July 1903, the Edinburgh branch of the party cancelled a meeting they had invited him to address. In his Oldham constituency, the Conservative Association told him that he would not be selected as their candidate in the next general election.

Churchill embarked on his first election campaign as a Liberal in 1906, visiting Bishopsthorpe, near York. He was elected as MP for a seat in Manchester with a majority of 1241.

CROSSING THE FLOOR

Anti-Churchill sentiment in Parliament solidified early in 1904 after he began to vote regularly against the Conservative government. The Liberals, sensing they were about to net the most dynamic new recruit the Commons had to offer, invited Churchill to stand as a candidate in north-west Manchester in the next election. Conservative fury escalated. On 29 March, when Churchill rose to speak in the Commons during a debate on the economy, the Conservative Prime Minister, Arthur Balfour, walked out of the Chamber, followed by his ministers and backbenchers.

Two days later, on 31 May, 1904, Churchill arrived in the House of Commons and briefly surveyed the government and opposition benches. After bowing to the Speaker of the House, a courtesy required of all MPs, he turned right, towards the Liberal benches. He took the same seat his father, Lord Randolph, had occupied during the Conservatives' years in opposition some 20 years earlier. Next to him sat David Lloyd George, the charismatic Liberal MP for Caernarvon.

Churchill had 'crossed the floor', as this switch of allegiance is known in Parliament. He had become not only a Liberal, but a supporter of the party's Radical wing, led by Lloyd George. Churchill's betrayal brought a fierce Conservative reaction. The grass roots of the Conservative Party, its clubs, were closed to him. He was pressured to resign from one club, the Carlton, where he had been a member for the last five years. Another, the deeply Conservative Hurlingham Polo Club, made an unprecedented move when its members blackballed Churchill, preventing him from becoming a member. It was the first time this had occurred in the club's history.

MINISTERIAL MATERIAL

Although he was a recent recruit, Churchill was recognised as ministerial material. The Liberals offered him a junior post as Financial Secretary to the Treasury in the new government of Sir Henry Campbell-Bannerman, elected in January 1906. Churchill turned it down. His tactic was shrewd, if opportunistic. At the Treasury, he would have been answerable to the formidable Herbert Asquith, Chancellor of the Exchequer, who cut an imposing figure in the Commons. By contrast, Victor Alexander Bruce, ninth Earl of Elgin and Secretary of State for the Colonies, was safely tucked away in the upper house, the House of Lords. Churchill requested, and was given, the post of Under Secretary at the Colonial Office. As Lord Elgin's junior in the lower house, he would have more independence and, with that, a larger share of the parliamentary limelight.

At the Colonial Office, Churchill at last had the opportunity to put some of his progressive ideas into practice. His first move was to push for a generous approach to the Boer republics in South Africa: the Transvaal and the Orange Free State. Churchill was determined that the Boer and British inhabitants should be treated equally. 'Do not let us do anything,' he wrote, 'which makes us

FROM CHURCHILL'S MAIDEN SPEECH IN THE HOUSE OF COMMONS, 18 FEBRUARY, 1901, DEALING WITH THE SITUATION OF THE BOERS AT THE END OF THE WAR IN SOUTH AFRICA

'I invite the House to consider which form of government, civil government or military government, is most likely to be conducive to the restoration of the banished prosperity … and most likely to encourage the return of the population now scattered far and wide. I understand that there are Hon. Members who are in hopes that representative institutions may directly follow military government, but I think they cannot realise thoroughly how very irksome such military government is …. Although I regard British officers in the field of war … as the best officers in the world, I do not believe that either their training or their habits of thought qualify them to exercise arbitrary authority over civil populations of European race. I have often myself been very much ashamed to see respectable old Boer farmers … ordered about peremptorily by young subaltern officers … I do not hesitate to say that as long as you have anything like direct military government, there will be … nothing but despair and discontent on the part of the Boer population and growing resentment on the part of our own British settlers.'

the champions of one race and consequently, deprives us for ever of the confidence of the other.'

Both republics were granted self-government later in 1906 and Boer governments were elected soon afterwards. 'The cause of the poor and the weak all over the world,' Churchill told the House of Commons, 'will have been sustained, and everywhere small peoples will get more room to breathe; and everywhere great empires will be encouraged by our example to step forward into the sunshine of a more gentle and more generous age.'

DUTY AND JUSTICE

Churchill's idealism was at the core of the Liberal principles in which he passionately believed. Lord Elgin, who was 25 years his senior, frequently found himself lectured by his junior minister. Some of Churchill's comments were so strongly worded that Elgin pasted white paper over them to conceal them from his officials.

'Our duty,' Churchill told Elgin, 'is to insist that the principles of justice and the safeguards of judicial procedure are rigidly, punctiliously and pedantically followed.' No case was too minor for Churchill to consider, particularly if it concerned abuse of justice. When the Governor of Ceylon (now Sri Lanka) found it too 'inconvenient' to bother about an appeal for reinstatement lodged by a former head guard on the railways, Churchill

'The cause of the poor and the weak all over the world will have been sustained ... everywhere great empires will be encouraged by our example to step forward into the sunshine of a more gentle and more generous age.'

Churchill in 1904, the year he 'crossed the floor' of the House of Commons to take his seat on the Liberal Party benches. This move earned him the mistrust of the Conservatives for the remainder of his parliamentary career.

told Lord Elgin: 'The Liberal Party cares very much for the rights of individuals to just and lawful treatment, and very little for the petty pride of a Colonial Governor.' On one occasion, Lord Elgin was himself berated by Churchill for refusing to take up a case his junior was anxious to pursue. 'In overruling me,' Churchill wrote, 'you do not assign any reasons, nor attempt to do justice to the very grave arguments I have so earnestly submitted to you.'

Churchill's zeal to confront head-on the injustices of the world irritated some of his colleagues. 'He is most tiresome to deal with, and I fear will give trouble – as his father did – in any position to which he may be called,' commented Sir Francis Hopwood, a senior civil servant at the Colonial Office. 'The restless energy, the uncontrollable desire for notoriety ... make him an anxiety indeed.'

THE MINIMUM STANDARD

Despite their disagreements, these feelings were not shared by the Earl of Elgin. At the end of 1906, when rumours were circulating that Churchill was in line to become the next President of the Board of Education, Elgin was concerned that he might lose his zestful junior minister. 'I have been dreading every (mail) to find the rumours true and that I was to lose your help,' Elgin told Churchill. Elgin was greatly relieved when the rumours came to nothing.

Churchill was already thinking of the future and of policies that lay beyond his Colonial Office remit. He had long been concerned about the poverty, squalor and insecurity of the working classes. In Britain's hierarchical society, sharply divided by class, there was little desire to change

CHURCHILL INSPECTS A NAVAL GUARD OF HONOUR IN 1908, THE YEAR OF THE DREADNOUGHT CONTROVERSY, A PARLIAMENTARY CONFLICT OVER HOW MANY OF THESE MIGHTY BATTLESHIPS BRITAIN WOULD NEED TO COUNTER THE STRENGTH OF THE KRIEGSMARINE, THE GERMAN NAVY. CHURCHILL AND LLOYD GEORGE BELIEVED FOUR WOULD BE SUFFICIENT, LEAVING ENOUGH FINANCE FOR SOCIAL REFORMS. THEIR CONSERVATIVE OPPONENTS WANTED EIGHT.

what was considered to be the natural order of things. But Churchill believed that the State should intervene to improve standards for workers and their families. So he devised a raft of new policies which he called the Minimum Standard.

The aim of the Minimum Standard was to bring an end to the exploitation of child labour and to set up labour exchanges where employers and people looking for work could contact each other. Working hours would be reduced to allow for reasonable leisure time. State benefits would be paid to mitigate the disastrous effects of unemployment on families. The policy also suggested a pensions system to protect people who were no longer able to work. These were radical ideas in the early 20th century and Churchill realised that they were bound to face strong resistance.

Fortunately he found a willing ally in Asquith, who replaced the ailing Campbell-Bannerman as Prime Minister in April 1908. Asquith was impressed by Churchill's ideas and his energy. He promoted Churchill to President of the Board of Trade, a post that offered him not only the chance

Clementine Hozier and Winston Churchill in their engagement photograph. It was a true love match and the pair remained close, calling each other the pet names Mr Pig and Mrs Pussycat.

Churchill arrives at St Margaret's, Westminster in London on 12 September, 1908 with his best man, Lord Hugh Cecil, for his wedding to Clementine. As a wedding present, Edward VII gave Churchill a gold-topped cane which he used for the rest of his life.

to promote his social reforms, but also valuable experience in industrial relations. Churchill took his place in Cabinet for the first time on 9 April.

DUMBSTRUCK

At 33, he was young for the position he had now attained. The pressures of high political office were considerable and what Churchill needed now was a supportive wife. He had already met a very promising candidate, the beautiful and intelligent Clementine Ogilvy Hozier. Their first encounter, at a society ball in 1904, was awkward. Churchill was dumbstruck by Clementine's striking looks and large, expressive

'Winston just stared. He never uttered one word and was very gauche – he never asked me for a dance, he never asked me to have supper with him ... he just stood and stared.'

eyes, which he later described as 'strange and mysterious'. Clementine recalled: 'Winston just stared. He never uttered one word and was very gauche – he never asked me for a dance, he never asked me to have supper with him ... he just stood and stared.'

Four years later, when they met again, Churchill, now a public figure of some importance, was more confident. He had long

ago realised that he would have to marry a woman who could tolerate his hectic lifestyle, mix easily with his influential friends and colleagues, and live with his appetite for action and excitement. Over the course of 1908, Churchill became convinced that, in Clementine Hozier, he had found the person who could combine the qualities he needed.

BLENHEIM PROPOSAL

As the grand-daughter of an earl, Clementine was socially on a par with Churchill, though her family history was unfortunate. Her father, Colonel Sir Henry Hozier, had deserted her mother, leaving her to bring up their three daughters in genteel poverty. The experience sharpened Clementine's character and gave her an understanding of ordinary life not often found in upper class women of the day. Clementine was also better

Clementine's marriage to Winston almost failed to take place. According to her daughter, Mary: 'She saw the face of the only real rival she was to know ... and for a brief moment, she quailed.' The rival was Churchill's political life which, according to Mary, 'laid constant claim to both his time and interest.'

educated than many of her contemporaries, for her circumstances had demanded that she be equipped to earn her own living.

In August 1908, Churchill invited Clementine to Blenheim Palace, his birthplace, which he saw as the ideal setting for a marriage proposal. For two days, he was unable to summon up the courage to ask her. On the third day his cousin Sunny, the Duke of Marlborough, came to his room, pulled him out of bed and told him to get on with it, or risk losing her. Churchill took Clementine for a walk in the palace gardens, where there was an ornamental Temple of Diana.

In this romantic setting, Churchill at last proposed and Clementine accepted. They were married at St Margaret's Church in Westminster a month later, on 12 September, and spent their honeymoon in Italy and Austria.

'I got married,' Churchill later wrote, 'and lived happily ever afterwards.' It was not quite true. Dynamic, restless and eager for new experiences, Winston Churchill was difficult to live with. There were quarrels, though never damaging, and Clementine needed frequent absences to gain respite from her husband's rollercoaster life. Unlike Churchill, who relished the excitement of public life, Clementine, with her streak of shyness, found the constant exposure difficult. All the same, there was no doubt that Winston and Clementine were true soul-mates. She soon became his closest friend and confidante and their marriage lasted 56 years.

Once the honeymoon was over and Churchill plunged back into the political fray, Clementine experienced the full force of the pressures of marriage to a public figure. In 1909 Churchill's social initiatives went through the parliamentary process that would turn them into law. They included old age pensions, national insurance against unemployment and ill-health, a minimum wage for the low paid and labour exchanges. As Churchill had expected, his policies provoked indignant protest and obstruction from the House of Lords. The main debate centred on the so-called 'People's Budget', which included proposals to pay for old age pensions by introducing heavy taxes on high incomes and a new tax on landed estates. The House of Lords opposed these measures, which they considered 'socialistic', and defeated the new budget outright by 375 votes to 75.

COMMONS AGAINST LORDS
Churchill unleashed a scathing attack on the House of Lords, employing the full force of his rhetoric. They were, he said, ' ... a played out, obsolete, anachronistic assembly, a survival of a feudal arrangement utterly passed out of its original meaning, a force long since passed away.'

The government confronted the House of Lords with a Parliament Act, which banned them from vetoing money bills and prevented them delaying any bill for more than two years. When the Lords resisted the bill, the king, George V, agreed to create up to 500 new Liberal peers to enable the legislation to be passed. The Lords, faced with the threat of being permanently swamped by a Liberal majority, gave in and on 10 August, 1911 they passed both the Parliament Act and the People's Budget.

PRISON REFORM

Churchill had already turned to new challenges. On 15 February, 1910, he had taken up a new appointment as Home Secretary. Churchill's first priority was to tackle the prison system which he considered unduly retributive, yet so ineffective that three-quarters of prisoners released at the

CHURCHILL ATTACKS THE ANTI-FREE TRADE CONSERVATIVE PARTY 31 MAY, 1905

We know perfectly well what to expect – a party of great vested interests, banded together in a formidable confederation, corruption at home, aggression to cover it up abroad ... the tyranny of a party machine; sentiment by the bucketful, patriotism by the imperial pint ... dear food for the millions, cheap labour for the millionaire.'

end of their sentences re-offended within a year. Churchill had never forgotten the frustration and shame of his own imprisonment by the Boers in 1899 and, uniquely among Home Secretaries, he was able to understand the experience from the prisoners' point of view. He set out to reduce sentences for less serious offences, provide better care for ex-prisoners, reduce the number of young people in jail and to furnish prisons with libraries and entertainments.

Churchill was the first Home Secretary to draw a distinction between criminal and political prisoners and between hardened criminals and occasional offenders. He was also meticulous in examining capital cases to see whether there could be any justification for reprieve from the death sentence. He even criticised individual judges for imposing punishments he thought unjust. One example was the case of a prisoner sentenced to seven years' penal servitude for stealing lime juice; another had been given seven years for stealing apples.

Winston Churchill, President of the Board of Trade, delivers a speech promoting his 1909 Budget at Saltburn, Yorkshire. This revolutionary plan aimed to improve the lives of the working class and the poor.

IN JANUARY 1911, POLICE
BESIEGED A HOUSE IN
SIDNEY STREET IN
LONDON'S EAST END,
WHERE TWO ARMED
ANARCHISTS WERE HOLED
UP. THE ANARCHISTS
EVENTUALLY DIED WHEN
THE HOUSE BURNED
DOWN. CHURCHILL (BY
THE GATE IN THE CENTRE),
THEN HOME SECRETARY,
WAS UNABLE TO RESIST
THE EXCITEMENT OF
WITNESSING THE ACTION
IN PERSON. HE WAS
AFTERWARDS CRITICISED
FOR PUTTING HIMSELF, A
MINISTER OF THE CROWN,
IN DANGER.

Churchill's approach to prison reform gave a cue for his critics, especially Conservative MPs, to accuse him of going soft on crime, and undermining the independence of judges. With his self-confidence and his strong sense of mission, Churchill dismissed the accusations as the kind of response to be expected of reactionaries still rooted in an age which had not understood the difference between justice and revenge.

Even so, Churchill found that there were pressures in dealing with the penal system which taxed even his fund of optimism and ebullience. Prisons, prisoners and punishments were intensely depressing and Churchill later admitted that, as Home Secretary, there was 'no post (which) I have occupied in government that I was more glad to leave.' 'We must not forget,' he later commented, 'that when every material improvement has been effected in prisons … when the proper food to maintain health and strength has been given, when the doctors, chaplains and prison visitors have come and gone, the convict stands deprived over everything that a free man calls life.'

Churchill was the first British Home Secretary to draw a distinction between criminal and political prisoners and between hardened criminals and occasional offenders.

TONYPANDY

Even more depressing for Churchill, certainly in the long term, was the crisis that occurred at Tonypandy in the Rhondda Valley, Wales, where a bitter dispute between mineowners and mineworkers over pay escalated into violent confrontation in November 1910. Police forces were brought in to halt the disorder, but the miners' resentment spilled over into rioting, the smashing of windows and looting. In despair, the Chief Constable of Glamorgan appealed directly to the army to send in 400 infantry and cavalry troops.

Although, as Home Secretary, Churchill was responsible for controlling the situation, he did not learn that the soldiers were on their way until mid morning on 7 November. He immediately sent orders for the military not to proceed to Tonypandy itself but to remain on standby. The infantry were halted at Swindon in Wiltshire, the cavalry much further on, at Cardiff. Instead, Churchill sent 200 constables and 70 mounted police from London to help deal with the trouble. As he later told the Commons: 'It must be the object of public policy to avoid collisions between

CHURCHILL CRITICISES THE HOUSE OF LORDS, 17 DECEMBER, 1909

The claim of the House of Lords is not that the electors, like the sons of distinguished men, may have legislative functions entrusted to them; it is that, whether they like it or not, the sons and the grandsons and the great-grandsons, and so on till the end of time, of distinguished men shall have legislative functions entrusted to them. That claim resolves itself into this, that we should maintain in our country a superior class, with law-giving functions inherent in their blood, transmissible by them to their remotest posterity and that these functions should be exercised irrespective of the character, the intelligence or the experience of the tenant for the time being and utterly independent of the public need and the public will.

On Churchill's orders, a detachment of the Lancashire Fusiliers was sent to the Rhondda Valley, Wales, to control rioting miners. Churchill's use of troops to settle industrial disputes would forever blight his relationship with the working classes.

troops and people engaged in industrial disputes.' On 8 November, Churchill offered to send a senior government industrial arbitrator to talk with the strikers. Three days later, the strikers accepted and met the arbitrator in Cardiff. Conservative newspapers furiously attacked Churchill for not sending in the troops and for going soft on what *The Times* termed 'a wild mob drunk with the desire of destruction.'

Unfortunately, the talks in Cardiff came to nothing and on 21 November the violence escalated. The strikers attacked the collieries and then moved into the village of Tonypandy where they wrecked 63 shops. The police finally managed to restore order, but one miner was killed, apparently from a blow on the head with a truncheon. Churchill eventually agreed to move the troops to Pontypridd, where the Aberdare and Rhondda valleys meet, and later sent troops into the Rhondda itself. They remained there for several weeks. The strikers were forced back to work on the mineowners' terms almost a year later, in October 1911.

AFTERMATH OF THE RIOTS

The events at Tonypandy inflamed Labour and trades union resentment towards Churchill and his initiatives aimed at improving life for the poor and underprivileged were soon forgotten.

Churchill was popularly dubbed an oppressor of the working classes. This reputation was fortified on 19 August, 1911, when striking railwaymen attacked a train at Llanelli, Wales, manhandled the engine driver, looted the trucks and mobbed a police station. This time, troops were ordered in by Churchill. In the subsequent melée, shots were fired and two civilians died.

Despite this, Llanelli did not inspire the same anti-Churchill fury as the events at Tonypandy, but for many years afterwards, among the Labour Party and the trades unions, Churchill was demonized with the cries 'Remember Tonypandy'. As late as 2000, 35 years after his death, Churchill's statue in Parliament Square was daubed with red paint during an anti-capitalist demonstration.

Fortunately for Churchill, his tenure as Home Secretary was brief. On 24 October, 1911, it was announced in Parliament that he had been appointed First Lord of the Admiralty. Churchill's long-held belief that Britain's best protection from outside attack was a strong Royal Navy was about to be put into practice.

WORLD WAR I

BETWEEN 1911 AND 1929, CHURCHILL EXPERIENCED HARSH
POLITICAL TIMES. AS FIRST LORD OF THE ADMIRALTY, HE WAS
HOUNDED FROM OFFICE IN 1915 OVER THE FAILURE OF THE
DARDANELLES CAMPAIGN. DURING THE GENERAL STRIKE OF 1926
HE EARNED THE HATRED OF MANY WORKING CLASS
PEOPLE. AFTER 1929, HE WAS OUT OF OFFICE AND
FAVOUR FOR THE NEXT TEN YEARS.

JUST OVER THREE MONTHS BEFORE Churchill was
appointed First Lord of the Admiralty, an incident
occurred on the Atlantic coast of North Africa which
demonstrated how his new role would place him at the
centre of international events. On 1 July, 1911 a
German gunboat, *Panther*, steamed into the port of
Agadir in Morocco, which lay within the French sphere
of influence. Ostensibly, the *Panther* was there to
protect local German commerce, but the French felt
threatened. The British government was convinced that the Agadir
crisis, as it came to be known, was only the first step in a move
towards a full-scale German naval presence in the area.

The scene was set for a confrontation that lasted well into the
autumn. The Royal Navy and the French fleet were placed on alert.
Plans to avert a German invasion of France were laid. The Germans
massed their fleet in the naval base at Kiel.

Eventually the Germans backed down, but for Churchill the
lessons were clear. Agadir, he was sure, was the portent of a coming
war with Germany. It reinforced Churchill's longstanding view that

*Churchill (on right) spent part of his brief World War I
service as commander of the 6th Royal Scots Fusiliers. He
earned such respect that nearly 55 years later, in 1965, a
contingent of Fusiliers formed the guard at his funeral.
Churchill (above) visited Lille on 27 October, 1918, as the
war was drawing to a close. He had been invited to tour
areas liberated by an Allied breakthrough four weeks earlier.*

the only way to protect Britain and its interests from the Germans was to make the Royal Navy invulnerable. Combative by nature, Churchill's standard reaction to threats was defiance. This attitude, which he amply demonstrated 30 years later, during World War II, was very much in evidence here.

At the Admiralty, Churchill embarked on a punishing programme of activity to ensure that the Royal Navy remained superior to the German Imperial Navy. Over the next two and a half years, he inspected dockyards and ships under construction. He visited naval barracks and the submarine school at Portsmouth. He scrutinised timetables for repairs, refits and the restocking of ships with ammunition and torpedoes. During this time Churchill lived and worked on board the Admiralty yacht *Enchantress*.

NEW DISTRACTIONS

Whatever time he managed to spend at home had to be snatched between engagements, but Clementine occasionally stayed with him on *Enchantress*. When she had to return home, both of them found separation painful. Winston and

Churchill enjoyed the popular aristocratic pastimes of hunting and shooting, and took part in this pheasant shoot in Yorkshire in 1910. He was confident in his handling of firearms, having proved himself adept with a pistol at Omdurman in 1898.

During army manoeuvres held on Salisbury Plain in 1910, Churchill was the guest of Sir John French (right), the future Commander-in-Chief of the British forces in France during World War I. After Churchill was removed as First Lord of the Admiralty over the Dardanelles failure, French tried to obtain command of a brigade in France for Churchill, but a jealous Lord Kitchener vetoed the idea.

Clementine were now the parents of two children – Diana, born on 11 July, 1909, and Randolph, their only son, born on 28 May, 1911. Churchill missed his family acutely. After his experience with his own distant father, he wanted to engage with his children and fretted when his contact with them was intermittent.

But his work at the Admiralty provided ample distraction. Churchill had a lifelong fascination with innovation and gadgetry. He was, for example, fascinated by Admiral John Fisher's

concept of a super-dreadnought battleship, an advance on Fisher's first dreadnought of 1906, which would be powered by oil instead of coal. The super-dreadnought, it was planned, would be able to reach a speed of 25 knots – 20 per cent faster than the dreadnought – and carry a powerful battery of eight 15-inch guns, where the dreadnought carried ten 12-inch guns. Churchill commissioned the first super-dreadnought, HMS *Queen Elizabeth*, in 1915 and instantly made all other naval ships obsolete. The super-dreadnought was one of the most revolutionary technological innovations of the early 20th century and it greatly strengthened the power of the Royal Navy.

Churchill was also enthralled by another equally exciting advance, aviation, and its potential as a new weapon of war. In 1911, only eight years after the Wright brothers' first pioneering flight, Churchill was already envisaging a naval air force that could bomb and machine gun enemy ground forces. Churchill not only tirelessly championed such a force, but became a keen enthusiast of aviation. He even started flying lessons early in 1913.

The assassination of the Austrian Archduke Franz Ferdinand and his wife by a Serbian nationalist on 28 June, 1914 ignited the conflict Churchill had long foreseen. Britain declared war on Germany on 4 August. Other countries followed until by early November the battle lines of World War I were drawn: the Allies – Britain, France and Russia – faced the Central Powers – Germany, Austria-Hungary and Ottoman Turkey.

THE CONFLICT WIDENS

At sea, the Royal Navy scored a first victory on 28 August by sinking three German cruisers in the Heligoland Bight in the North Sea. The British Grand Fleet anchored in Scapa Flow, north of Scotland, blocking access to the Atlantic so that the much feared German battleships were holed up in harbour. But despite the blockade there were still naval losses. The Germans sank three Royal Navy cruisers in September 1914, in the North Sea near the Dogger Bank, and three more

Churchill (centre) was First Lord of the Admiralty in September, 1913, when he attended army manoeuvres in Buckingham. Churchill, his brother John (right) and his close friend Sir Ian Hamilton (left) had been together during the war against the Boers in South Africa.

were torpedoed by German submarines in October and November.

The news on the Western Front in France and Belgium, where the British and French armies were in retreat, was no better. By October the fighting in France had settled into trench warfare: an atrocity of waste, squalor and death festooned with barbed wire. A pall of depression hung over the British war effort. One of the first tasks of the War Council created by the Prime Minister, Asquith, in December 1914 was to repair damaged morale. Another was to open a second front to end the stalemate in Flanders.

The most promising opportunity appeared to be an attack on Ottoman Turkey, the weakest of the Central Powers. Churchill developed plans to destroy the forts lining the Dardanelles, the 45-mile-long strait linking the Aegean Sea and the Sea of Marmara, which guarded the Ottoman capital, Constantinople. By securing the strait, Churchill hoped to force Turkey out of the war and to open up a route to Russia. A joint Anglo-French fleet of 15 battleships launched the assault in mid February 1915. Two heavy bombardments silenced most of the Turkish forts, but then things began to go wrong. Three Allied battleships exploded and sank: the Turks had mined the straits. Five more battleships ran into another undetected minefield; three sank and two were disabled. Turkish howitzers positioned along the Dardanelles shoreline destroyed a ninth battleship.

DISASTROUS LANDINGS

The naval assault on the Dardanelles had failed and the fleet was withdrawn. The military results were no better. The landings that took place on the Gallipoli peninsula in the Dardanelles on 25 April were a disaster. At one of the landing

CHURCHILL ON THE ROYAL NAVAL AIR SERVICE, 10 NOVEMBER, 1913

I would venture to submit ... that the enduring safety of this country will not be maintained by force of arms unless over the whole sphere of aerial development, we are able to make ourselves the first nation .... The keenest eye, the surest hand, the most undaunted heart, must be offered and risked and sacrificed in order that we may attain – as we shall undoubtedly attain – that command and perfection in aerial warfare which will be an indispensable element, not only in naval strength but in national security.

DAVID LLOYD GEORGE
(LEFT) WAS A STAUNCH
SUPPORTER OF
CHURCHILL (RIGHT)
WHEN HE BECAME
EMBROILED IN
CONTROVERSY
SURROUNDING THE
DARDANELLES CAMPAIGN
IN 1915–1916.
CHURCHILL WAS HEAVILY
CENSURED FOR THE
COSTLY FAILURE OF THE
CAMPAIGN, WHICH
EARNED HIM THE
DESCRIPTION 'THE
BUTCHER OF GALLIPOLI'.

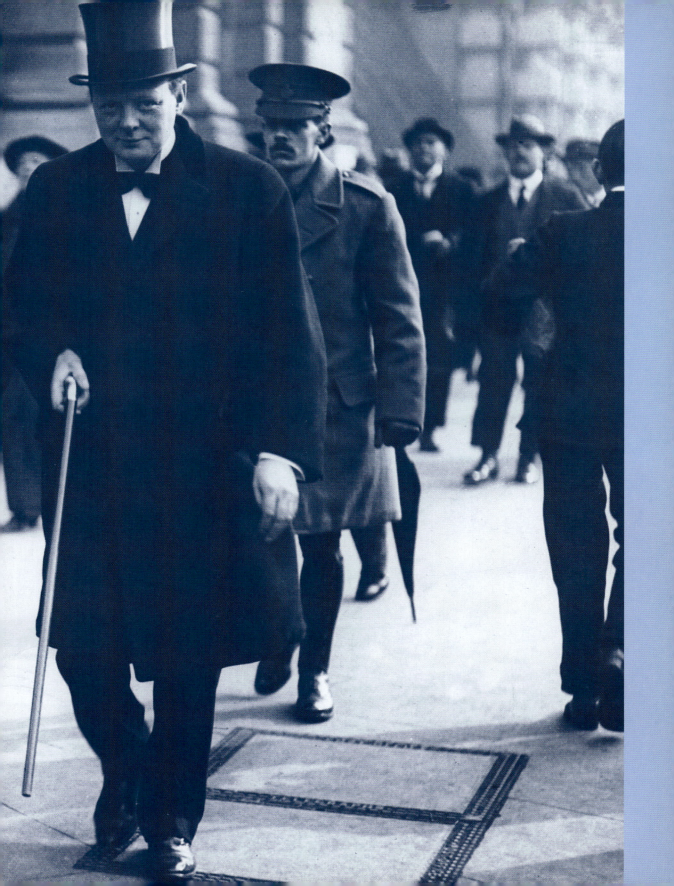

beaches, Allied troops – including a large number of men from the Australian and New Zealander Army Corps (ANZAC) – found themselves pinned down as the Turks raked the shoreline with machine-gun fire. They gained some ground but were soon driven back again by ferocious Turkish counter-attacks. Months of bloody fighting followed, with a heavy cost in lives, before further landings were made at the beginning of August. These also failed.

By the end of 1915 the Allies were forced to admit defeat. Some 252,000 Allied troops, more than half of those who took part, were killed or injured before the survivors were evacuated in January 1916. The loss of so many lives for neither gain nor glory had a profound effect on the public mind and the names 'Dardanelles' and 'Gallipoli' became synonymous with the savagery and waste of war. Churchill was haunted by the episode for many years afterwards and it precipitated his political downfall.

The Conservatives seized on the opportunity to punish Churchill for deserting the party and, as they saw it, flaunting the political heights he attained under the Liberals. The Dardanelles disaster provided the perfect stick with which to beat Churchill, and in 1915 his political enemies made the most of it.

DISILLUSIONED

At the start of the war, the two political parties had agreed to a truce for the sake of national unity. In the summer of 1915, Asquith decided to form a coalition government but the Conservatives made one stipulation: Churchill must be removed from the Admiralty. Asquith needed the Conservatives more than he needed Churchill, so Churchill was demoted to the

> **'Feet and clothing breaking through the soil, water and muck on all sides and about this scene in the dazzling moonlight, troops of enormous bats creep and glide ... '**

largely peripheral post of chancellor of the Duchy of Lancaster. Although the position enabled Churchill to remain in the government, with a seat on the War Council, he became severely depressed. Clementine observed his anguish in the raw. 'I thought he would die of grief,' she recalled.

That summer Churchill settled with his family at Hoe Farm, near Godalming in Surrey, a quiet retreat where his bruised ego found a measure of peace and calm. He took up painting, first in watercolours, later branching out into oils. It became a lifelong interest, one that Churchill later described as a 'wonderful cure and a means of forgetting all vexations'. But throughout 1915 the newspapers kept the Dardanelles controversy alive. *The Times* commented darkly on Churchill's 'disquieting personal adventures' and greed for power. The criticisms fed a charge that, as First Lord, Churchill had flagrantly overruled his naval advisers on the War Council.

Churchill hoped that Asquith would defend him in the House of Commons, but the Prime Minister failed to do so. By October 1915 Churchill had become totally disillusioned. He felt he needed to leave England, even though it would part him from his wife and children, who by now included another daughter, Sarah, born on 7 October, 1914.

Churchill resigned from the government and rejoined the army. In late October, he left for the

Churchill addresses munitions workers in Enfield, Middlesex in 1915. Two years later he was appointed Minister of Munitions. He used his position to influence military strategy and tactics in every way he could.

Churchill in 1916 during his military service in France. That year, on July 1, an Allied offensive near the River Somme had cost the lives of 20,000 British soldiers on the first day alone. Churchill was appalled by the news, believing that victory could not be achieved 'simply by throwing in masses of men on the Western Front'.

front in Flanders where he experienced at first hand the squalor and horrors of war in the trenches. 'Graves dug into the defences and scattered about promiscuously,' he wrote to Clementine. 'Feet and clothing breaking through the soil, water and muck on all sides and about this scene in the dazzling moonlight, troops of enormous bats creep and glide, to the unceasing accompaniment of rifles and machines and the venomous whining and whirring of the bullets which pass overhead.' But the war provided welcome relief for Churchill from the stress he had recently suffered. He wrote: 'I have found happiness and content such as I have not known for many months.'

The stalemate of the trenches was totally at odds with the daring, fast-moving warfare Churchill had known in India, the Sudan and South Africa. Churchill's vivid imagination and his penchant for unconventional gadgetry prompted him to suggest a way in which men could advance out of the trenches without being blown to pieces by German artillery and machine-gun fire. He envisaged a huge metal shield moved along by wheels or caterpillar tracks and equipped with a flame-thrower and two or three Maxim machine-guns. Only a direct hit from a field gun could halt the advance of this shield which would be heavy enough to crush the barbed wire that fronted the trenches. Churchill sent a memorandum outlining his idea to his friend F E Smith, and Smith agreed to circulate it among members of the Cabinet. Churchill's idea for an armoured trench-crossing machine was one of many proposed at the time in an effort to reduce the appalling slaughter of trench warfare. An innovation along similar lines to Churchill's idea was the tank, designed by the engineers Walter Wilson and William Tritton in 1915–16. The British first used the tank on 15 September, 1916, during the five-month-long Battle of the Somme.

OSTRACISED

Asquith's political demise began to look likely in 1916, when he lost an argument in Parliament over conscription into the armed forces. Despite the high casualty rate, which eventually made full conscription unavoidable, Asquith had clung to the hope that the army could be maintained as a volunteer force. In France, Churchill could see why this was impossible. The 6th Royal Scots Fusiliers, the infantry battalion he commanded, suffered such appalling casualties that its survivors had to be absorbed by another unit.

CHURCHILL ON WORLD WAR I, 11 SEPTEMBER, 1914

We did not enter upon the war with the hope of easy victory; we did not enter upon it in any desire to extend our territory, or to advance and increase our position in the world; or in any romantic desire to shed our blood and spend our money in Continental quarrels. We entered upon this war reluctantly after we had made every effort compatible with honour to avoid being drawn in, and we entered upon it with a full realisation of the sufferings, losses, disappointments, vexations and anxiety and of the appalling and sustaining exertions which would be entailed upon us by our action. The war will be long and sombre (but) we entered it and entered it rightly, with the sure and strong hope and expectation of bringing it to a victorious conclusion.

Churchill's enthusiasm for flying was so great that he would grab any opportunity he could to take to the air, as at Portsmouth in 1915 when he took a flight in an army biplane.

Left without a military command, Churchill returned to Parliament where his first task was to clear himself of blame for the Dardanelles campaign. He quickly realised how difficult that was going to be. He was openly insulted in the House of Commons, where his speeches were punctuated by cries of 'What about the Dardanelles?' In the Conservative press his

'ghastly blunders' were repeatedly examined. Conservative MPs openly ostracised him.

Stung into action, Churchill insisted on an exhaustive enquiry into the handling of the Dardanelles campaign. A Royal Commission was appointed and, as Churchill had hoped, its members exonerated him. Instead, they pointed the finger at Asquith for approving every stage of the campaign, and at Kitchener, who was now dead, for his indecision and neglect. Asquith resigned in December 1916 and was replaced by David Lloyd George.

Although Lloyd George wanted Churchill in his cabinet, there were obstacles preventing his return to ministerial office. Conservative hatred of Churchill still burned hot and strong. The Tory press claimed that Churchill lacked judgement. In Parliament, Lord Curzon, one time Viceroy of India and a member of the War Cabinet, called him 'an active danger in our midst'. The situation was saved by an act of magnanimity from Dr Christopher Addison, the Minister of Munitions. Addison's admiration for Churchill was so profound that he gave up his post so that Churchill could succeed him. The appointment went through on 24 July, 1917.

Churchill's charm was among his greatest assets, and did much to explain the loyalty he inspired. One of his first tasks as Minister of Munitions was to settle a strike at the important Beardmore munitions works on the Clyde outside Glasgow in Scotland. The strikers' leader, David Kirkwood, was invited to London to talk the problem over. Expecting a hostile reception, Kirkwood was amazed when Churchill greeted him warmly and offered him tea and cakes. Before long, they had worked out an acceptable answer to problems no one else had been able to solve in the 18 months since the strike started.

Churchill tackled the challenges of his new position with great gusto. He streamlined his Ministry and galvanised armament factories to higher production. He liaised with the French and Americans, who had entered the war in 1917, to coordinate the supply of guns and shells to the armies at the front.

World War I came to an end with the armistice signed on 11 November, 1918. Four days later, Clementine gave birth to her fourth child, Marigold Frances, but a General Election was imminent and Churchill could spend only a short time with his third daughter. He was re-elected Member of Parliament for the safe seat of Dundee, a seat he first won in May 1908, with a large majority of 15,365 votes and became Secretary of State for War and Air in Lloyd George's coalition government.

World War I had convulsed Europe as never before, but the upheavals did not end with the armistice. At the war office, and afterwards in his role as Colonial Secretary from 1921, Churchill was closely involved in the dramas that ensued. In Ireland, the British Army was locked in conflict with the Republican nationalist movement. The British brought in the 'Black and Tans', auxiliary police recruited from ex-soldiers, to attempt to suppress the terror tactics used by the Irish Republican Army (IRA). The Black and Tans' methods were brutal, but Churchill soon realised the IRA could not be overcome by force. So, in October 1921, he engaged in talks with Michael Collins, an IRA leader. They made a treaty to create an Irish Free State, partitioning Ireland into a Catholic South and a Protestant North. Unfortunately, this failed to resolve the crisis and the struggle continues to this day.

> **Churchill's finances ... were often depleted by his extravagance. He had a taste for cigars and oysters, and drank champagne at almost every meal, accompanied by plenty of claret throughout the day.**

PERSONAL TRAGEDIES

Ireland was not Churchill's only worry. As Colonial Secretary with responsibility for the new Middle East department, Churchill found religious disputes of a very different kind. Palestine had long been a part of the Ottoman Empire, but after World War I, it came under British rule. Although the territory was largely settled by Arabs, it was historically regarded by the Jews as their homeland. The Jews longed to retrieve it and the

British government pledged support for their aim with the Balfour Declaration in 1917. Churchill, a confirmed Zionist, was tasked with overseeing the immigration of Jews into Palestine. The loss of land was bitterly resented by the Arabs and the resultant hostilities were to continue unabated.

As Churchill was tussling with these problems, he was struck by two personal tragedies. His mother Jennie fell downstairs and broke her ankle. Gangrene developed and Jennie died on 23 June, aged 67. Only two months later tragedy struck again when Marigold, Churchill's youngest daughter, developed meningitis. She died on 24 August, aged only two and a half. Churchill was distraught. 'It seemed so pitiful,' he wrote to a friend, 'that this little life should have been extinguished just when it was so beautiful and so happy, just when it was beginning … '

A month before the end of World War I in 1918, Churchill visited munitions factories in the north of England and raised the spirits of the female workers (below) on his tour of the factory yards.

Churchill (right) had become a champion polo player while serving in India from 1896–1898, and played for the Commons polo team (on the left of the photograph) against the Lords in 1925. The Commons won.

OUT OF PARLIAMENT

Clementine gave birth to her fifth and last child, another daughter, Mary, just over a year later on 15 September, 1922. The same day, Churchill paid £5000 for Chartwell Manor, a large, rambling country house in Kent. Churchill loved Chartwell, though Clementine, who was less fond of rural life, never truly liked it. Her antipathy was partly due to its great expense, the equivalent of a year's income from Garron Towers, the estate in Northern Ireland that Churchill inherited from a distant cousin in 1921.

Garron Towers gave a welcome boost to Churchill's finances, which were often depleted by his extravagance. He had a taste for cigars and oysters, and drank champagne at almost every meal, accompanied by plenty of claret throughout the day. The upkeep of Chartwell was a further drain and a new threat emerged in October 1922, when the wartime coalition came to an end after seven years. Lloyd George was obliged to resign, along with his government. The Conservatives won the general election that followed on 12 November and to his dismay Churchill, who was out of action after an operation for appendicitis, was defeated in his Dundee constituency. 'In the twinkling of an eye,' he later wrote, 'I found myself without an office, without a seat and without an appendix.'

Out of Parliament for the first time in more than 20 years, Churchill decided to take a salutary break from politics. 'After ... years of rough official work,' he remarked, ' ... there are many things worse than private life.'

He supervised the rebuilding of Chartwell, holidayed with his family in the south of France and started work on a history of World War I. Entitled *The World Crisis*, his war memoirs were published over ten years. The first volume

CHURCHILL AFTER HIS REMOVAL AS FIRST LORD OF THE ADMIRALTY, 5 JUNE, 1915

I have borne the burden of being ... responsible to Crown and Parliament for all the business of the Admiralty and when I say responsible, I have been responsible in the real sense, that I have had the blame for everything that has gone wrong ... the archives of the Admiralty will show in the utmost detail the part I have played in all the great transactions that have taken place. It is to them I look for my defence.

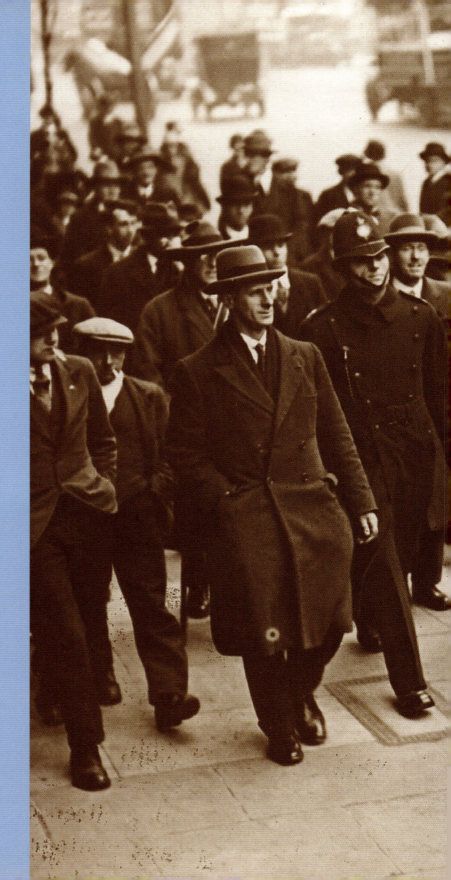

CHURCHILL WALKS TO
PARLIAMENT TO DELIVER
HIS 1927 BUDGET.
AS CHANCELLOR OF
THE EXCHEQUER,
CHURCHILL MADE SOME
CONTROVERSIAL
DECISIONS. IN 1925,
UNDER PRESSURE FROM
CONSERVATIVE
ECONOMISTS, HE
RETURNED BRITAIN TO
THE GOLD STANDARD, A
MONETARY SYSTEM
WHICH FIXES EXCHANGE
RATES. THIS HAD
DISASTROUS
CONSEQUENCES, RAISING
THE COST OF EXPORTS,
CRIPPLING INDUSTRY
AND PAVING THE WAY
FOR THE GENERAL STRIKE
OF 1926.

CHURCHILL ON THE END OF WORLD WAR I, 16 DECEMBER, 1918

The war is won .... We have reached the end of the long, long trail. And what a victory! .... In the five weeks which have passed since firing stopped on the Western Front, I have felt a new and fresh inward satisfaction every day in contemplating the magnitude and the splendour of our achievement and our success .... It fills our hearts with pride and with thankfulness that we have lived in such a time and belong to such a race.

Churchill enjoyed hunting and participated in a boar hunt in France in 1928, organised by the Duke of Westminster. He was accompanied by his 17-year-old son Randolph (left) and Mlle 'Coco' Chanel (centre), who later became a pioneering couturier.

the Liberal and Labour parties, who had 350 seats between them. Within months Baldwin was forced to resign and was replaced by James Ramsay Macdonald, leader of the Labour Party. Britain's first Labour government took office but as a minority administration, dependent on Liberal support.

Churchill, who failed to win a seat in the election, was alarmed. The Bolshevik revolution of 1917 was still recent history and had given him a lifelong hatred of communism. He was convinced that the new Labour government would prove similar to the regime in Russia and leave 'a dark and blighting shadow on every form of national life.'

His fears were shared by many Liberal MPs but Churchill doubted they could put up an effective opposition and began to consider

appeared in April 1923, the second six months later. A review in the *New Statesman* considered that Churchill himself played too much of a starring role: 'He has written a book which is remarkably egotistical.' Margot Asquith, wife of the former Prime Minister, was more complimentary: 'I think your book a great masterpiece,' she told Churchill, advising him to stick to writing and painting, and to 'lie low: do nothing in politics'.

But Churchill found it impossible to stay out of politics for long, particularly at a time when fundamental change was working its way into the fabric of Parliament. The Liberals' halcyon days were over, and they were split into factions – one of them aligned with the Conservatives, the other with the rising Labour Party. This put a question mark over Churchill's own political future. As long as he remained a Liberal, it was unlikely that he would be offered a government post.

HATRED OF COMMUNISM

Churchill needed to secure another seat in Parliament but this was no simple task in the political climate of the time. When the ailing Andrew Bonar Law resigned as Prime Minister in 1923, his successor, Stanley Baldwin, called a general election that proved disastrous for the Conservatives. The party secured 258 seats, 100 less than before the election. They became a minority government, at risk of being outvoted by

CHURCHILL ON SOCIALISM AT BATTERSEA TOWN HALL, LONDON, 11 DECEMBER, 1925

The follies of Socialism are inexhaustible. They talk of comradeship and teach the brotherhood of men. What are they? They are the most disagreeable people. Talk about worldwide common brotherhood! Even among themselves, they have twenty discordant factions who hate one another even more than they hate you and me .... Can you not feel a sense of disgust at the arrogant presumption of superiority of these people?

On polling day, 30 May, 1929, Churchill and Clementine took to the streets to meet and greet supporters in his Epping constituency. Churchill was re-elected, but his party, the Conservatives, were beaten by Labour.

BACK IN THE CABINET

A week later Stanley Baldwin, Prime Minister once again, asked Churchill to become his Chancellor of the Exchequer. Churchill was delighted, and later wrote that when Baldwin offered him the second most important post in government, he wanted to reply in slang terms with 'Will the bloody duck swim?' He thought the better of it. 'As it was a formal and important conversation,' Churchill went on, 'I replied: "This fulfils my ambition. I still have my father's robe as Chancellor. I shall be proud to serve you in this splendid Office."'

Churchill had rejoined the Conservative Party after an absence of 20 years, but the compassionate mindset that had made him a pioneering social reformer in the past was unchanged. In his first budget as Chancellor, he outlined his plans for pension schemes for widows and orphans, and reduced from 70 to 65 the age at which the payment of old age pensions should begin. A 10 per cent tax reduction would come into force to help families on the lowest incomes.

Many Conservatives saw Churchill's ideas as state interference rather than state aid. They became even more uneasy with his proposals for solving a dispute in the mining industry. Faced with falling profits, the mine owners had decided to reduce workers' wages and in retaliation, the National Union of Mineworkers was threatening strikes. The situation had reached a deadlock. Churchill's solution to the crisis was to pay a government subsidy to mine owners so that wages need not be cut. The mineowners agreed, but nine months later they told Baldwin that their losses were still so great that subsidy or no subsidy, wages must be reduced. A state of emergency was declared. At midnight on 3 May, some 2.5 million workers

changing parties once more. Stanley Baldwin grabbed the opportunity to woo Churchill back to the Conservative Party and other disaffected Liberals with him. Churchill failed to win a seat as an Independent candidate in a by-election in March 1924 but six months later Baldwin found him a safe Conservative seat at Epping in north-east London.

The Labour government lasted only eight months, foundering on sensational press reports about the 'Red Menace' and accusations linking the party to the creeping tide of communism. In the general election that followed on 29 October, 1924, Churchill won Epping with a handsome majority of more than 9000 votes. The Conservatives returned to power with a majority of 223 seats over the other two parties. In the same poll, the Liberals slumped to a mere 40 seats.

across the country obeyed a call for a general strike put out by the Trades Union Congress.

Over the nine days the strike lasted, volunteers, mainly from the middle class, went to work to keep Britain going. Students drove buses and lorries delivering food and other essential supplies. Retired managers and ex-army officers acted as special constables. Troops, sometimes accompanied by tanks, guarded public buildings and stood by to deal with any trouble.

CONCILIATION FAILS

Churchill took command of a special news-sheet, the *British Gazette*, issued by the government while the newspapers were on strike. His purpose was to dissipate public fear and encourage reconciliation between the mine owners and workers but his role

in the strike simply increased the hostility of organised labour towards him.

The General Strike left behind a bitter aftermath. The miners were finally forced back to work by hunger, destitution and the onset of winter. Churchill's skills as a conciliator had failed and despite his genuine concern for the welfare of the working classes – which was to influence all of the five budgets he produced as Chancellor of the Exchequer between 1925 and 1929 – he was now viewed as their arch-enemy. Churchill was also out of favour with his Conservative colleagues, who disagreed with his intervention in the running of private business.

On 30 May, 1929 Churchill and the rest of the Conservative government discovered to their chagrin just how much progress Labour had made now that the Liberal Party had ceased to be a credible opposition in Parliament. In the General Election held that day, the Labour Party was once more returned to power as a minority government, with 288 seats in the Commons, to the Conservatives' 260 and the Liberals' paltry 59. Churchill was re-elected MP for Epping but once again he had lost his government post. The next would not come his way for another ten years.

Churchill and daughters Sarah (left) and Mary helped to build a house in the grounds of his Chartwell estate in Kent in 1928. Churchill was so skilled that he received honorary membership of the local bricklayers' union.

THE WILDERNESS YEARS

DURING THE 1930S, CHURCHILL WAS OUT IN THE POLITICAL COLD. HE BECAME INCREASINGLY CRITICAL OF THE GOVERNMENT'S POLICY OF APPEASEMENT OF THE NAZI REGIME IN GERMANY, CONVINCED THAT THE NAZIS WERE INTENT ON CONQUEST. HE WAS PROVED RIGHT ON 3 SEPTEMBER, 1939, WHEN HOSTILITIES BEGAN WITH THE GERMAN INVASION OF POLAND.

ALTHOUGH THE MINORITY STATUS of the new Labour government gave Churchill hope that, together, Conservatives and Liberals would be able to spike its guns, the Conservative leader, Stanley Baldwin, did not share his priorities.

In July 1929, nationalists were making trouble in Egypt, a British protectorate, but the Labour Party seemed unwilling to deal with the situation: British troops were withdrawn from Cairo to the Suez Canal, and the High Commissioner, Lord Lloyd, was ordered home. Lloyd enlisted Churchill's help to retrieve his position, but Baldwin did not believe that Egypt was an issue on which Labour could be fruitfully challenged. When Churchill put Lloyd's case to the House of Commons, Baldwin sat stone-faced in his seat and the Conservative benches put up a barrage of heckling.

Once again, Churchill found himself isolated from the rest of the Conservative Party. In 1904, when he 'crossed the floor', he had provoked anger over his perceived disloyalty to the Conservative leadership. In 1929 history had repeated itself. But this second time,

Churchill's penchant for Havana cigars (above) was a habit he acquired during his time in Cuba in 1895. Churchill (left) at Chartwell in February 1939. In Parliament this same month, the Prime Minister Neville Chamberlain referred to him as 'Bogey No. 1'.

he was out of office, and more vulnerable to Conservative criticism.

INDIAN NATIONALISM

Egypt was not the only source of contention. On 30 October the Conservative shadow cabinet agreed to support the Labour government's plan to give India dominion status within the British Commonwealth, which granted a measure of self-government but not full independence, as demanded by Indian nationalists. Churchill still felt it conceded too much. He had always regarded the Empire as a benevolent and civilising influence, and was convinced that the Indians were not ready to govern themselves. He had some cogent reasons: centuries of sectarian hatred between Hindus and Muslims showed no signs of fading. Rioting and murder, including the killing of British officials, continued even as dominion status was being discussed in London.

Churchill was not the only Conservative to have doubts. Another was Neville Chamberlain, the future Prime Minister, who believed it would take 50 years or more before the Indians were ready to govern themselves. But the argument was already

lost. Baldwin made known his support of Labour's policy and, unwilling to be exposed as disloyal by opposing their leader, Conservatives fell into line. To Churchill's dismay, the procedures needed to implement dominion status went forward, endorsed towards the end of 1931 by a vote in Parliament of 369 for the government to only 43 against. Four years later, in 1935, the process culminated in the India Bill, which contained the provisions to convert India from a colony into a dominion.

NEAR-FATAL CRASH

In 1931 the second Labour government foundered over its plan to impose a 10 per cent cut in unemployment benefit. Several Labour ministers refused to accept the cuts and, faced with defections, the government resigned on 24 August, 1931. This might have been an opportunity for a Liberal-Conservative partnership, as advocated by Churchill, to take power, but that prospect was lost when the three main political parties united in a National Government. The new coalition scored a handsome victory in a General Election on 27 October, winning 530 seats. Churchill's majority at Epping almost doubled, but in Parliament he was out in the cold: he was not offered a place in the new government.

Churchill had other pressing concerns. The collapse of the US stock market on Wall Street, New York, in October 1929 had snowballed into a worldwide economic recession, wiping out the fortunes of thousands of people across the world. Churchill himself had suffered heavy losses in the crash which he needed to recoup. In 1931, *The World Crisis: The Eastern Front*, the last volume of his war memoirs, was published and sold well. He negotiated a contract for another lecture tour of the United States, which guaranteed him at

CHURCHILL ON MAHATMA GANDHI, THE INDIAN NATIONALIST LEADER, 23 FEBRUARY, 1931

We ought to dissociate ourselves ... from any complicity in the weak, wrong-headed and most unfortunate administration of India by the Socialists .... It is alarming and also nauseating to see Mr Gandhi, a seditious Middle Temple lawyer, now posing as a fakir of a type well known in the East, striding half-naked upon the steps of the viceregal palace, while he is still organising and conducting a defiant campaign of civil disobedience, to parley on equal terms with the representative of the King-Emperor.

At the time of this informal Conservative rally in 1930, Churchill had been out of office for 15 months, since the election of May 1929. He was increasingly isolated within the Conservative Party due to his opposition to the granting of dominion status for India.

least £10,000, and the *Daily Mail* newspaper agreed to pay him £8000 for a series of articles on life in the United States.

Then, just as his financial future seemed assured, his life was thrown into disarray. On 13 December, while on a lecture tour in the United States, Churchill suffered a terrible accident. He was walking along Fifth Avenue in New York when he stepped out into the road without checking the traffic and was struck by a car. He suffered serious injuries to his head and legs, and spent three weeks recuperating in New York and another three in the Bahamas. Never one to miss a good subject for an article, he wrote an account of his accident for the *Daily Mail*, which was

syndicated around the world. Letters of sympathy flooded into the newspaper's offices. Churchill was impatient to get back to work and despite a bout of pleurisy and severe inflammation of the nerves in his arms and shoulders, he returned to the lecture circuit in January 1932. In three weeks, he gave lectures in 19 US cities, earning £7500, double what a British Prime Minister received in a year.

THE RISE OF NAZISM

Churchill arrived home in Britain on 17 March, and in April he was once again embroiled in controversy. In 1919 he had opposed the harsh provisions of the Versailles Treaty, which had fixed

THE DAILY MIRROR, Friday, January 1, 1932.

HAPPY NEW YEAR TO ALL OUR READERS

Daily Mirror

Wireless on Page 16

THE DAILY PICTURE NEWSPAPER WITH THE LARGEST NET SALE

No. 8,770 | Registered at the G.P.O. as a Newspaper. | FRIDAY, JANUARY 1, 1932 | One Penny

£20,000 FREE INSURANCE

SEE PAGES 3 AND 20

HOW *YOU* BENEFIT BY *OUR* INSURANCE

IN NEW YEAR HONOURS

BATTERED—NOT SHATTERED

Lieutenant - Colonel Wilfrid William Ashley, M.P., former Minister of Transport, one of the five new Barons.

Mr. Leifchild (Leif) Stratton Jones, M.P. for Camborne Division of Cornwall 1923-24 and 1929-31, who is made a Baron.

Annie Viscountess Cowdray, who is made a Dame Grand Cross of the Order of the British Empire in the New Year Honours, which are made known this morning.

Miss Margaret Tuke, formerly principal of Bedford College, becomes a Dame Commander of the Order of the British Empire.

Mr. Reginald Clifford Allen, treasurer and chairman of the Independent Labour Party 1922-26, who receives a Barony.

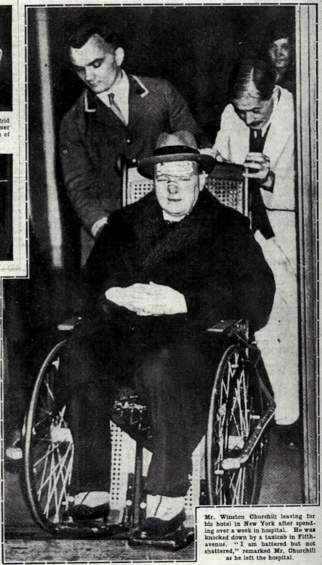

Mr. Winston Churchill leaving for his hotel in New York after spending over a week in hospital. He was knocked down by a taxicab in Fifth-avenue. "I am battered but not shattered," remarked Mr. Churchill as he left the hospital.

a programme of punitive reparations for the vanquished Germany at the end of World War I. The treaty had also enforced drastic reductions in the German armed forces and banned the possession of tanks and heavy artillery. Churchill had predicted that these onerous demands would cause fierce resentment and by 1932 the truth of his warning was becoming apparent.

Churchill made the headlines (left) on New Year's Day in 1932 after he was knocked down by a car in New York and badly injured.

Churchill (below) was elected as Chancellor of Bristol University on 13 December, 1929. He was the longest-serving chancellor of the 20th century: his term lasted 36 years, until his death in 1965.

The opportunistic leader of the rising National Socialist party, Adolf Hitler, was able to capitalise on the bitterness of the German nation about the perceived wrongs of Versailles. Hitler promised to retrieve lost territories and restore Germany's power and influence. After failing to seize power by violent means in Munich in 1923, Hitler instead used Germany's new democratic system of government. By late 1932, after a series of elections, the Nazis became the largest single party in the *Reichstag*, the German Parliament. On 30 January, 1933, Adolf Hitler was appointed Chancellor of Germany by the venerable, but reluctant, President Paul von Hindenberg, with Franz von Papen as his Vice-Chancellor. Von Papen and Hindenberg believed they could control Hitler, but it was not long before they realised how gravely mistaken they were.

At Chartwell in July 1931, Churchill entertains guests including Charlie Chaplin (far right). The pair met when Churchill was in Hollywood in 1929. Churchill promised to produce a film starring Chaplin as the young Napoleon Bonaparte, but nothing came of the idea. Also present at Chartwell were (from left) Tom Mitford, Clementine's cousin, Clementine, holding hands with her eldest daughter Diana, and her son Randolph.

Churchill's daughter Diana marries her second husband, Duncan Sandys, MP. Diana was a tragic figure: both her marriages failed, and she suffered bouts of depression before committing suicide in 1963.

In Britain, an entirely different ethos was prevalent. The horrors and tragic waste of World War I, which had left few families untouched, were still fresh in people's minds and pacifist sentiment dominated British policy. But this desire for peace was not the only reason for the government's policy of appeasement. In Britain the Great Depression of the 1930s had given rise to mass unemployment, near-destitution, business failures, a slump in industry and a widespread feeling of gloom and hopelessness. The government's main priority was to ensure industrial recovery and it was unwilling to

jeopardise this by ploughing money into defence and armaments. There was also remorse for the punitive reparations the Germans were made to pay and the war guilt they were forced to bear under the terms of the Versailles Treaty. Adolf Hitler, whom Churchill considered so dangerous, was viewed in quite another light by those who were more afraid of communist Russia. They saw Nazi Germany as the antithesis of communism, and a protection against it.

In this light, the policy of appeasing Hitler, which was supported by George VI himself, seemed a just means of salving the conscience of the victors on the one hand, and providing an insurance policy on the other. Churchill had more pragmatic, but also more sombre views. He had witnessed the new, militant Germany at first hand in July 1932, when he visited the country to research a biography of his ancestor John Churchill, the first Duke of

Marlborough. He saw the battlefield of Blenheim, where Marlborough had defeated the French and Bavarian armies in 1704. But Churchill also witnessed Germans, both young and old, whipped up to a frenzy of nationalist and antisemitic fervour by Hitler's rabble-rousing speeches.

Churchill was re-elected MP for Epping on 15 November, 1935, but failed to win a position in the new Conservative government. The MP Nancy Astor warned Baldwin that putting him in government 'will mean war at home and abroad'.

'AN ALARMIST WARMONGER'

Back in England, Churchill told the House of Commons on 23 March, 1933: 'When we read about Germany, when we watch with surprise and distress the tumultuous resurgence of ferocity and war spirit, the pitiless ill-treatment of minorities … the denial of the normal protections of civilised society to large numbers of individuals solely on the grounds of race – when we see that occurring in one of the most gifted, learned, scientific and formidable nations in Europe, one cannot help feeling glad that the fierce passions that are raging in Germany have

not found, as yet, any other outlet (but) Germans.'

While he was in Germany, efforts to arrange a meeting between Churchill and Hitler had been made by Ernst Hanfstaengel, a friend of Churchill's son, Randolph. Hitler, it seems, was not interested. 'What part does Churchill play?' asked the Führer. 'He is in opposition and no one pays any attention to him.'

Not many wanted to listen. Churchill was labelled alarmist and a warmonger for insisting that disarmament must not be carried out while Germany remained dangerous. 'The removal of the just grievances of the vanquished ought to

Churchill had no qualms about doing labouring work, such as mending the roof at Chartwell. He delighted in his practical skills and found the work therapeutic. He also built a wall on his Chartwell estate, laying up to 200 bricks in a day.

precede the disarmament of the victors,' Churchill told the House of Commons in November 1932. 'To bring about anything like equality of armaments … while those grievances remain unredressed would be almost to appoint the day for another European war – to fix it as if it were a prize fight.'

REARMAMENT URGED

Churchill's opponents in Parliament had already dismissed him as a lone voice in the wilderness. But he was not to be diverted. One of his major concerns was the government proposals to reduce spending on the Royal Air Force and to close down one of four flying schools. He was aware that the development of aircraft in World War I and later technological advances had made fundamental changes in the scope of aerial warfare. Aircraft could now bomb and machine-gun towns and cities from the air, putting civilians at great risk.

Secret intelligence reports from the British air attaché in Berlin revealed that the Nazis had violated a ban on military aircraft imposed at Versailles and were actively rearming. This was accomplished through secrecy and subterfuge. For example, Lufthansa, the German passenger airline, was used as camouflage for the development of aircraft for the Luftwaffe, the German air force. Gliding and flying clubs trained pilots who would later fight in World War II. Artillery guns were constructed, their barrels disguised as factory chimneys. Tanks were made to look like farm tractors and motor torpedo boats like pleasure craft.

Churchill did not have access to Cabinet and Foreign Office intelligence, but he had his own grapevine of informants – civil servants, army and Royal Air Force officers – who shared his anxieties. The risks these officials ran were enormous. By giving Churchill access to secret intelligence, they were disobeying the Official Secrets Act, and were therefore putting their careers on the line, even risking imprisonment. But by this means Churchill learned of deficiencies in aircraft development and pilot training, and of shortages of gas masks, weapons, ammunition, armoured cars, tanks, lorries and many other items essential for national defence. Constantly and tirelessly he used his clandestine knowledge to tax the government over these shortfalls.

'To bring about anything like equality of armaments ... while those grievances remain unredressed would be almost to appoint the day for another European war ... '

SECRET INFORMATION

Churchill's earliest informant was Major Desmond Morton, a former colleague at the War Office. Morton headed a government intelligence unit that kept track of the movement of raw materials used

---

CHURCHILL ON WAR IN THE AIR, 7 FEBRUARY, 1934

This cursed, hellish invention and development of war from the air has revolutionised our position. We are not the same kind of country we used to be ... only twenty years ago .... It is not merely a question of what we like and what we do not like, of ambitions and desires, of rights and interests, but it is a question of safety and independence .... I cannot conceive how, in the present state of Europe and of our position in Europe, we can delay in establishing the principle of having an Air Force at least as strong as that of any Power that can get at us .... To have an Air Force as strong as the airforce of France or Germany, whichever is the stronger, ought to be the decision which Parliament should take, and which the National Government should proclaim.

In June 1937 Churchill named a
new railway engine the 'Royal Naval
Division' at Euston, London. The
division, made up of naval volunteer
reserves, was formed by Churchill at
the outbreak of World War I.

sole executive power in Germany
as both Chancellor and President.
In March 1935, he repudiated
the disarmament clauses of the
Versailles Treaty. Hitler also
revealed that Germany was
rearming and that he had
recreated the German air force,
the Luftwaffe.

PREDICTIONS OF DEVASTATION

Churchill persevered in his
campaign to impress on a
complacent Parliament not only
the Nazi preparations for war, but
also the enormity of their
persecutions of Jews, gypsies,
homosexuals and other minorities.
The House of Commons
continued to ignore him. Churchill

for armaments by Germany and other European
countries. Churchill first contacted Morton in the
spring of 1933. From then on, he used Morton's
information to strengthen his arguments against
disarmament. Churchill was not entirely alone. The
Secretary of State for War, Douglas Hogg, Lord
Hailsham, had similar forebodings, but Hailsham,
like Churchill, was labelled a scaremonger and his
warnings were ignored.

On 14 October, 1933, Nazi Germany
withdrew from the League of Nations and the
International Disarmament Conference, which
had first met at Geneva, Switzerland, in 1927.
On 3 August, 1934, a day after the death of the
aged President von Hindenburg, Hitler assumed

may have failed to shift government ministers from
their pacifist stance, but he certainly disturbed
them with the accuracy of his facts. Late in 1934,
Desmond Morton passed him a detailed analysis
of the Nazis' air plans. The National Government
had by then already agreed a new programme to
build up the Royal Air Force, which was to be
completed by 1939. But Churchill wanted it
finished much sooner and decided to use Morton's
information to bolster his appeal in Parliament.
Churchill delivered his speech in the House of
Commons, painting a horrific picture of the effects
of intensive enemy bombing of London and other
British cities. A week's persistent bombing of
London, he predicted, would kill or maim up to

40,000 people. Incendiary bombs would incinerate whole districts. Millions of people would be forced to flee for safety to the open countryside.

Churchill received an ovation: his campaign to alert Parliament to the Nazi danger was gaining him followers. But Baldwin obfuscated, denying that the Luftwaffe strength was anywhere near that of the Royal Air Force.

Churchill was a genial, talkative host, and Chartwell was often full of celebrity visitors. In 1939 he entertained the eminent physicist Albert Einstein.

In April 1935, another civil servant from the Foreign Office, Ralph Wigram, arrived unexpectedly at Chartwell. Wigram brought with him some damning facts: these revealed that German aircraft factories were already stepping up production in preparation for war. Wigram returned to Chartwell the following week with more worrying statistics. These proved that the Luftwaffe already possessed a first-line strength of 800 aircraft, whereas the equivalent figure for the RAF was only 453.

On 22 May, in a defence debate in the Commons, Stanley Baldwin, then Lord President

of the Council, confessed that his estimate of Luftwaffe strength had been wrong. At last, Churchill seemed to be making progress.

In June 1935, the ailing Prime Minister Ramsay MacDonald resigned in Baldwin's favour. There was no official position for Winston Churchill in the new Cabinet but despite their clashes, Baldwin admired Churchill and offered him a place on the Air Defence Research Sub-Committee. Churchill's close friend Professor Frederick Lindemann was a

... If there is going to be a war – and no one can say that there is not – we must keep him fresh to be our war Prime Minister.'

fellow member. A distinguished, if sometimes abrasive, Oxford academic, Lindemann encouraged Churchill's interest in cutting-edge invention. At his first Sub-Committee meeting on 25 July, Churchill was fascinated to learn details of a new facility for detecting enemy aircraft by radio-location: the first experiments with radar, as it was later termed, had been successful.

In a General Election held on 14 November, the Conservative Party returned to power with a landslide victory that gave them a majority of 280 seats in the House of Commons. Churchill hoped that he might be offered a place in Baldwin's government. For almost a week, he waited at Chartwell for a telephone call offering him a position but none came.

In 1937, while in France, Churchill produced an oil painting of the chateau at St Georges-Motel. He found art therapeutic. Painting, he said, 'is a wonderful cure, because you cannot really think of anything else.'

CHURCHILL ON WAR WITH NAZI GERMANY, MARCH 1936

Germany ... fears no one. She is arming in a manner which has never been seen in German history. She is led by a handful of triumphant desperadoes ... Very soon they will have to choose ... a war which could have no other object and which, if successful, can have no other result than a Germanized Europe under Nazi control. Therefore, it seems to me that all the old conditions present themselves again, and that our national salvation depends upon our gathering once again all the forces of Europe to contain, to restrain and if necessary to frustrate, German domination.

KEPT IN RESERVE
Churchill was disappointed, but he had misinterpreted Baldwin's motives. Sensing the threatening turn of events, Baldwin believed that Churchill was destined for a much more distinguished future. 'I feel we should not give him a post at this stage,' he wrote, ' ... If there is going to be a war – and no one can say that there is not – we must keep him fresh to be our war Prime Minister.' For the moment, though, Churchill was still playing the outsider and the thorn in the government's flesh.

In March 1934, Churchill had suggested to Maurice Hankey, the Cabinet Secretary, that a Ministry of Defence should be created. Two years later, in February 1936, Hankey discussed the appointment of a Defence Minister with Sir Warren Fisher, Permanent Secretary to the Treasury. Fisher felt the post should go to a man 'with no axe to grind, or desire to make a place for himself'. This description did not fit Winston Churchill. Instead the conscientious but insipid Sir Thomas Inskip, the Attorney General, was offered the post. Inskip fitted the brief perfectly. As Neville Chamberlain commented, 'Inskip would create no jealousies. He would excite no enthusiasm but he would involve us in no fresh perplexities.'

Churchill (left) formed a close friendship with the Prince of Wales – later Edward VIII. His outspoken support of Edward during the abdication crisis of 1936 attracted criticism in the Commons from those who felt he had ulterior motives. Churchill also misjudged the mood of the British public, who were strongly opposed to a marriage between the King and an American divorcee, Mrs Wallis Simpson.

'OUTRAGEOUS EVENTS'

Churchill was alarmed. He predicted that the Nazis were on the war path and within six months could invade France through Belgium and Holland, which would put them in a position to threaten Britain. Czechoslovakia, Austria, Poland and the Balkan and Baltic states would also be imperilled. Fortunately, more than six months would pass before Churchill's prophecy came true.

Churchill's predictions were gradually gaining an audience. His support came not only from serving officers, but also MPs who were at last waking up to his warnings. Sir Robert Vansittart, Permanent Under-Secretary at the Foreign Office, was on Churchill's side and other Foreign Office officials were following Ralph Wigram's lead. In May 1936, they arranged for Churchill to address the Anti-Nazi League, which had been formed to counteract Nazi propaganda.

During 1936, it became increasingly apparent that a crisis in Europe was in the making. After Hitler's shock news about German rearmament the previous year, no action had been taken against the Nazi regime. In 1936, Hitler tested Britain and France to see how much further he could go. He started with the Rhineland, the region between Germany and France that had been demilitarised in 1919. On 7 March, 1936, German troops marched in and garrisoned the Rhineland, but again, this action produced no response.

Churchill (right) with Brendan Bracken, an Irishman who was his staunch supporter in the 1930s and later became a cabinet minister in his wartime government. Like Churchill, he strongly opposed appeasement.

In August 1939, only weeks before the start of World War II, Churchill toured the Maginot Line which had been built along France's border with Germany. The French believed that the Line was impenetrable. Churchill, here with the French General Alphonse Georges, was not convinced.

Neville Chamberlain, another champion of appeasement, succeeded Baldwin as Prime Minister at the end of May 1937. Soon after the Nazis' remilitarisation of the Rhineland, Churchill had told the pro-German Charles Vane-Tempest-Stewart, seventh Earl of Londonderry: 'If I read the future aright, Hitler's government will confront Europe with a series of outrageous events and ever growing military might.' The first of Hitler's 'outrageous events' occurred on 12 March, 1938, with the *Anchluss*, the integration of Austria into Nazi Germany, which was forbidden by the Versailles Treaty. Next, Hitler began to make threats over the alleged maltreatment of ethnic Germans living in the Sudetenland of Czechoslovakia.

Six months after the *Anchluss*, on 29 September, Neville Chamberlain and the French

Prime Minister, Edouard Daladier, flew to Munich for two days of negotiations with Hitler. The settlement they made was hailed as a triumph of appeasement. The two Prime Ministers agreed that Hitler could absorb the Sudetenland into German territory without consulting the Czech government. Chamberlain returned to England to be greeted at Hendon airport by crowds cheering his claim to have secured 'peace for our time'. 'The fools,' Daladier commented when he received the same wild reception in Paris.

Hitler had promised at Munich that the Sudetenland would be his last territorial demand. Less than six months later, on 15 March, 1939, Nazi troops occupied the rest of Czechoslovakia. After another three months, Hitler began to pressure Poland with demands to return two territories taken from Germany after World War I: the free city of Danzig and the Polish Corridor which gave the land-locked Poles access to the sea.

'WINSTON IS BACK!'

In the summer of 1939, a campaign was under way in the newspapers in Britain to bring Churchill back into government. Some junior ministers took up the theme to demand that he be made War Minister. Chamberlain was not keen. He hoped the campaign would peter out, and the Poles would concede the territories to Hitler. But the Poles refused Hitler's demands.

On 23 August, 1939, to the rest of the world's amazement, Nazi Germany and Communist Russia signed a mutual non-aggression pact. Two ideological enemies, fundamentally opposed in almost every respect, had become allies and a menace to the rest of Europe. Chamberlain, his hopes ruined, was heartbroken.

Churchill leaving Downing Street on the afternoon of 1 September, 1939, the day the forces of Nazi Germany invaded Poland. 'The die is cast,' Chamberlain commented. Two days later war was declared on Germany.

CHURCHILL ON THE MUNICH AGREEMENT, 5 OCTOBER, 1938

Our loyal, brave people ... should know that there has been gross neglect and deficiency in our defences; they should know that we have sustained a defeat without a war, the consequences of which will travel far with us along our road; they should know that we have passed an awful milestone in our history, when the whole equilibrium of Europe has been deranged, and that the terrible words have for the time being been pronounced against the Western democracies: 'Thou art weighed in the balance and found wanting.' And do not suppose this is the end. This is only the beginning of the reckoning. This is only the first sip, the first foretaste of a bitter cup which will be proffered to us year by year unless by a supreme recovery or moral health and martial vigour, we arise again and take our stand for freedom.

Two days later, Britain signed a treaty of alliance with Poland, promising support should the Nazis attack. On 1 September, 1939, German troops invaded. An unstoppable *blitzkrieg*, or lightning war, swept through the country, scattering the Polish resistance. Britain and France demanded that the Germans withdraw but their protests went unheeded. Chamberlain was left with only one possible course of action. In a radio broadcast at 11:15AM, on Sunday, 3 September, he informed the British people that they were once again at war with Germany.

That same day, Chamberlain offered Churchill a place in the War Cabinet as First Lord of the Admiralty. Soon afterwards the Board of Admiralty signalled all Royal Navy ships: 'Winston is back!'

Churchill's wilderness years were over, but World War II, so long predicted, so greatly feared, had begun.

FINEST HOUR

Back in power as First Lord of the Admiralty in 1939, and Prime Minister in 1940, Churchill needed all his resolve for the awesome tasks that lay ahead. He had to overcome the defeatist attitudes of others and lead the nation through a fight for its very survival. By mid 1940, Britain was standing alone before the might of Nazi Germany.

Winston Churchill entered the First Sea Lord's office at the Admiralty at 6:00PM on 3 September, 1939, seven hours after Britain declared war. Nearly 25 years had passed since he left the Admiralty in 1915. 'So it was that I came again to the room I had quitted in pain and sorrow … ' he wrote later. 'Once again, we must fight for life and honour against all the might and fury of the valiant, disciplined and ruthless German race. Once again! So be it!'

Although daunting, it was an exciting prospect for Churchill. At 65, he had reached an age at which other men could expect to enjoy the sunset years that followed a lifetime of work. But Churchill's real work was only just beginning.

The challenge he faced in his second term at the Admiralty was formidable. He soon discovered that Britain was dangerously ill-prepared for war. Factories had not been mobilised fast enough. There were critical shortfalls in the supply of munitions, weaponry, up-to-date equipment for the army and modern aircraft for the Royal Air Force (RAF). Shipbuilding for the navy had been neglected, creating a shortage of capital ships to provide escorts for battleships.

Churchill (left) inspects the surviving officers and crew of HMS Hardy, sunk at Narvik on 10 April, 1940. His return to Cabinet office as First Lord of the Admiralty made headline news (above) on 4 September, the day after the war began.

BRITAIN'S FIRST DAY OF WAR: CHURCHILL IN NEW CABINET

Meanwhile, in Poland, the Germans were demonstrating how quick and crushing their victory could be. Six armoured and eight motorised divisions smashed the antiquated Polish forces while the Luftwaffe destroyed the railways and shot the Polish air force out of the sky. On 17 September the Soviets activated their non-aggression pact with Germany, and Soviet forces invaded from the east. By the end of September, the country had been carved up between them.

On 1 October Churchill made his first wartime broadcast. He spoke of the fate that had overtaken Poland which had a history of being invaded and conquered by Germany and Russia. 'Poland,' he told his audience, 'has been again overrun by two of the great powers who held her in bondage for 150 years but were unable to quench the spirit of the Polish nation. The heroic defence of Warsaw shows that the soul of Poland is indestructible and that she will rise again like a

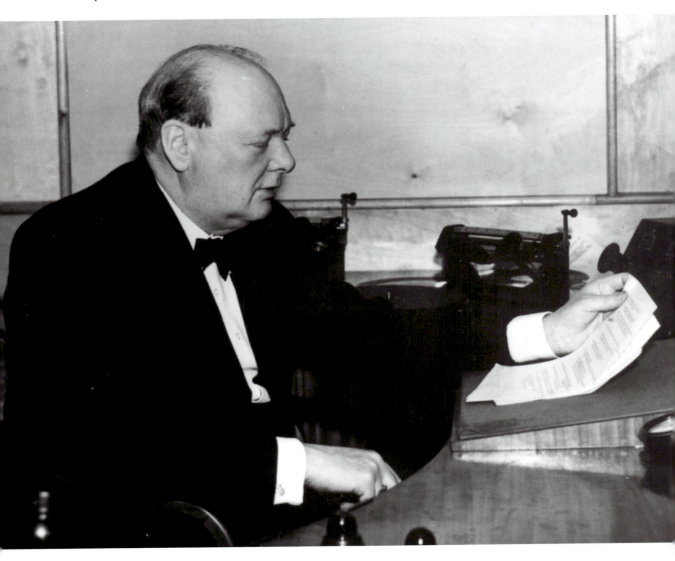

rock, which may for a spell be submerged by a tidal wave, but which remains a rock.'

NARVIK PLAN

Churchill galvanised the Admiralty staff with a constant flow of ideas. He was willing to consider any measure, any theatre of conflict, any even half-promising idea that might enable Britain to put up effective resistance to the Nazis. On the second day of the war, he suggested that the French army, backed by the RAF, should mount an attack on the West Wall, the Germans' western line of defences, to divert their attention from Poland. Eight days later, he was fielding a plan to send two battleships to bombard the German Baltic coast. A week later Churchill was proposing to cut off the Germans' supply of Swedish iron ore, which was transported via the Lapland Railway and the port of Narvik. If the navy could lay mines inside Norwegian territorial waters, the iron-ore carriers would have to divert away from Narvik and out to sea, where British ships would be waiting for them.

Churchill's scheme had the backing of the Admiralty but he came up against resistance from Chamberlain. Chamberlain's attitude, wrote Dr Thomas Jones, a former Deputy Secretary to the Cabinet, 'was costive and dull ... (He) talks of endurance and victory in the most defeatist tones.'

By contrast, Churchill always appeared confident, though he never promised miracle solutions. His speeches in Parliament and broadcasts were realistic and hopeful but also defiant. His broadcast of 1 October, in which he spoke of the threat to Britain from German submarines, demonstrated his approach. 'I speak as First Lord of the Admiralty with special caution,' Churchill began. 'It would seem that

The first of Churchill's many wartime radio broadcasts was made on 1 October, 1939. He dealt with the U-boat menace in the Atlantic, the pact recently concluded by Nazi Germany and Soviet Russia, and the plight of Poland.

CHURCHILL ON THE OUTBREAK OF WAR, 3 SEPTEMBER, 1939

We must not underrate the gravity of the task which lies before us, or the temerity of the ordeal .... We must expect many disappointments and many unpleasant surprises .... The Prime Minister said it was a sad day, and that is indeed true, but at the present time there is another note which may be present, and that is a feeling of thankfulness that, if these great trials were to come upon our island, there is a generation of Britons here now ready to prove itself not unworthy ... of those great men, the fathers of our land, who laid the foundations of our laws and shaped the greatness of our country.

the U-boat attack upon the life of the British Isles has not so far proved successful. It is true that when they sprang out upon us and we were going about our ordinary business ... they managed to do some serious damage. But the Royal Navy has immediately attacked the U-boats and is hunting them night and day .... We must, of course, expect that the U-boat attack upon the seaborne commerce of the world will be renewed presently on a greater scale. We hope, however, that by the end of October we shall have three times as many hunting craft at work ... and we hope that ... our means of putting down this pest will grow continually.' The war, Churchill warned, might last for as long as three years, but Britain would fight to the end, 'convinced that we are the defenders of civilisation and freedom'.

REFUSAL TO NEGOTIATE

Unlike many of his colleagues, Churchill did not shy away from danger. When, on 5 October, 1939, Adolf Hitler indicated his readiness to negotiate peace with Britain and France in exchange for recognition of German dominance over Poland and Czechoslovakia, some ministers, including the Foreign Secretary, Lord Halifax, were tempted to bargain. Churchill refused even

The marriage of
Randolph Churchill
(fourth from left)
and Pamela Digby
(third from the left)
took place on 4
October, 1939. When
Churchill was told
that the young
couple did not have
enough money to
marry, he replied:
'What do they need?
Cigars, champagne
and a double bed!'

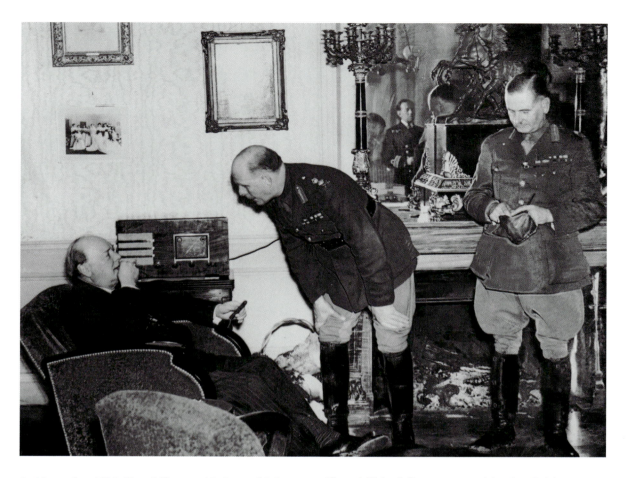

In November 1939 Churchill met with General John Gort (centre), Commander-in-Chief of the British Expeditionary Force, which was defending the Franco-Belgian border. The BEF was formed after the Boer War as a small unit for rapid overseas deployment. But by May 1940, it had 10 infantry divisions, a tank brigade and an RAF detachment of some 500 aircraft.

to consider negotiations unless reparations were made to the conquered peoples and their 'effective life and sovereignty' were restored.

Churchill was determined that the war against Germany should be prosecuted with steady resolve. But other Cabinet ministers seemed unable to commit themselves to a definite course of action. They vacillated over Churchill's plan to mine Norwegian waters and put British military units ashore at Narvik until January 1940, when, four months after

Churchill had first suggested it, the Cabinet finally rejected his scheme.

Churchill was incensed. On 15 January, he wrote to Lord Halifax of the 'awful difficulties which our machinery of war-conduct presents to positive action. I see such immense walls of prevention ... that I wonder whether any plan will have a chance of climbing over them ... victory will never be found in taking the line of least resistance.'

The supine attitude of the Chamberlain government was no more acceptable to the British public than it was to Winston Churchill. Mrs Violet Pearman – 'Mrs P', as Churchill called her – had worked as his secretary before the war and she expressed a widespread opinion when she wrote to him: 'I think the country relies on you ... to express national feeling in the only way that Germany understands, standing up to the bully and proving him the coward that he is.'

INDECISION AND DELAY

Chamberlain appeared incapable of 'standing up to the bully' himself. On 2 April, 1940, he gave a speech suggesting that the Nazi Führer had waited too long to act after his conquest of Poland, while the pace of Britain's rearmament was on the increase. Hitler, Chamberlain claimed, 'has missed the bus'. Events were to prove otherwise. A week earlier, Churchill's much-delayed Narvik initiative had at last been sanctioned. The campaign was due to start on 8 April, but it did not proceed as expected. The mining of Norwegian waters went ahead, but the next day, on 9 April, German forces landed at several places along the Norwegian coast. Neighbouring Denmark was overcome the same day. Meanwhile, German airborne forces captured Oslo, the Norwegian capital, and the port of Stavanger.

British and French troops managed to get ashore at Narvik, and the Norwegians, with the help of the Allied forces, put up dogged resistance, but their efforts were doomed to failure. The Allied enterprise had come too late.

Churchill was infuriated that the Narvik expedition had been sabotaged by indecision and delay. He was not alone. On 29 April, a group of

In January 1940, Churchill met the French General Alphonse Georges (right), who was in command of the Northeast front in France and was responsible for liaison with the British forces in the area. Churchill was concerned about the inferior equipment used by the French army and the nonchalant attitude shown by its commanders.

senior Members of Parliament confronted Halifax with a strong protest about the 'want of initiative' the government had shown not only over Norway, but in every other area of policy since the war had begun. Even Chamberlain's longstanding and loyal supporters turned against him. Thoroughly rattled, Chamberlain tried to cling on to his position by telling the House of Commons that Britain retained the 'balance of advantage' in Norway. This was demonstrably untrue and on 7 May, when he arrived at the Commons to take part in a debate on Norway, Chamberlain was jeered with ribald cries of 'Missed the bus! Missed the bus!'

> 'At last I had authority to give directions over the whole scene. I felt as if I were walking with destiny, and that all my past life had been but a preparation for this hour and for this trial.'

After two days of stormy debate, the government scraped a narrow victory, but the verdict proved unacceptable. There was uproar in the Commons and loud demonstrations against the Prime Minister – an unprecedented event in Parliament. Chamberlain could no longer ignore the calls for his resignation.

WALKING WITH DESTINY

Already, Churchill had emerged as the front runner to succeed him but Chamberlain shrank from leaving the premiership in the hands of a man he still regarded as an unreliable troublemaker. Chamberlain's choice was Lord Halifax. Halifax was unwilling, and had his own suggestion: 'Winston,' he said, 'would be a better choice.'

Then suddenly the picture changed. On 10 May the German armies invaded Belgium, the Netherlands and France. In a repeat performance of their Polish campaign nine months earlier, the German *blitzkrieg* began pounding, strafing and bombing the three countries into submission. Chamberlain decided, and Churchill loyally agreed, that in this new crisis a change of leadership was unwise.

When the news spread that Chamberlain was going to remain in place, many Conservative MPs were outraged. But it was the Labour opposition that decided the issue. In a Cabinet meeting, at which Chamberlain presided, he received a message that no member of the Labour Party would serve under him as Prime Minister. Less than an hour later, Chamberlain tendered his resignation to George VI at Buckingham Palace.

That evening, Churchill was summoned to the palace. 'I suppose you don't know why I have sent for you,' the king said in a bantering

CHURCHILL ON THE SOVIET INVASION OF POLAND, 1 OCTOBER, 1939

We could have wished that the Russian armies should be standing on their present line as the friends and allies of Poland, instead of as invaders …. I cannot forecast to you the actions of Russia. It is a riddle, wrapped in a mystery inside an enigma; but perhaps there is a key. That key is Russian national interest. It cannot be in accordance with the interest or the safety of Russia that Germany should plant itself upon the shores of the Black Sea, or that it should overrun the Balkan States … That would be contrary to the historical life-interest of Russia.

tone. Churchill, on the brink of attaining the summit of all his ambitions, gave a similarly artless reply. 'Sir,' he told the king, 'I simply couldn't imagine why.' 'I want to ask you to form a government,' the king said with a smile.

A 1940 poster encourages people to invest their money in war bonds to aid the British war effort. The cost of the war was enormous, consuming 55.3 per cent of national expenditure at its peak in 1943.

Churchill felt profound relief. 'At last I had authority to give directions over the whole scene,' he wrote later. 'I felt as if I were walking with destiny, and that all my past life had been but a preparation for this hour and for this trial.'

The challenges awaiting him were stupendous. Every day, Churchill and his 'Grand Coalition' – as he named the all-party government he headed – were confronted by new crises and fresh threats. The forces of Nazi Germany surged through the Low Countries and France like an irresistible tide.

The Dutch were forced to surrender after only four days, on 14 May. The Belgians clung on, but their situation was increasingly grave.

Churchill had hoped that the seemingly formidable French army would be able to hold off the Nazi *blitzkrieg*, but their defences were failing and they were rapidly losing the will to fight on. Despite the proximity of the fighting and the personal risk involved, Churchill flew to France twice in three days in mid June 1940, hoping to persuade the French High Command not to give up the struggle. He even offered to create a union between Britain and France to strengthen their resistance. However, all Churchill's urgings proved useless. The French will to win faded fast and Paul Reynaud, the French Prime Minister, informed Churchill that his government might shortly have to ask the Germans for an armistice. At this point, Churchill's emotions proved too much for him: he sat listening to Reynaud with tears streaming down his face.

On 8 May, 1940, two days before he became Prime Minister, Churchill (left) walked to the Houses of Parliament for a debate on the situation in war-torn Norway, accompanied by Admiral Sir Alfred Dudley Pound (right), the First Sea Lord.

The men of HMS Exeter returned to Britain in February 1940 to a hero's welcome. In the Battle of the River Plate, off Uruguay, the Exeter had forced the superior German battleship Admiral Graf Spee into Montevideo, where the ship was scuttled.

TENACIOUS ATTITUDE

The fall of France would have grave consequences for Britain, exposing the island to the threat of invasion by forces poised less than 21 miles across the English Channel. Churchill never shirked the truth, however terrifying it might be, when he spoke of the prospects that lay ahead. 'It would be foolish ... to disguise the gravity of the hour ... we must expect that as soon as stability is reached [in France], the bulk of that hideous apparatus of aggression ... will be turned upon us .... There will be many men and many women in this island who, when the ordeal comes upon them, as come it will, will feel comfort and even a pride, that they are sharing the perils of our lads at the Front – soldiers, sailors and airmen – and are drawing away from them a part ... of the onslaught they have to bear .... Our task is not only to win the battle, but to win the war.'

At this stage Churchill was still dogged by some Members of Parliament who disagreed with his tenacious attitude. One of them was Neville Chamberlain, who was now Lord President of the Council. He told a secret War Cabinet meeting that 'while we would fight to the end to preserve our independence, we were ready to consider decent terms if such were offered to us.' Churchill was furious: 'Nations which went down fighting,' he warned the Cabinet 'rose again, but those who surrendered tamely were finished.'

DEFIANCE AND DETERMINATION

Getting his message of defiance across to the Americans was another difficulty Churchill had to face. Since the end of World War I, more than 20 years previously, the United States had adopted a predominantly isolationist policy. This echoed one of the provisions of the Monroe Doctrine of 1823, which decreed that the United States

Churchill (left) looks out to sea from the deck of a Royal Navy destroyer during his visit to a port in the north of England. The exact location of many pictures taken in wartime was not disclosed.

On the morning of 10 May, 1940, hundreds of German troops were dropped by parachute near Rotterdam, The Hague, Moerdijk and Dortrecht in the Netherlands. They quickly gained control of the country.

should not become involved in European wars and political conflicts. Even though the American President, Franklin Delano Roosevelt, did not share the unwillingness of many Congressmen to become embroiled in European quarrels, isolationist influence was for the moment too strong to be ignored.

Churchill sent a telegram to Roosevelt on 15 May that set out the situation in Europe in frank terms, while tacitly asking for American aid. 'If necessary', Churchill told Roosevelt, 'we shall continue the war alone, and we are not afraid of that. But I trust you realise, Mr President, that the voice and force of the United States may count for

nothing if they are withheld too long. You may have a completely subjugated Nazified Europe established with astonishing swiftness … '

Churchill went on to request the use of 50 US destroyers from World War I that had been mothballed in American naval shipyards. Although he stressed that these destroyers were crucial to Britain's survival, President Roosevelt refused: his advisers feared that if Britain were overrun, their destroyers would fall into Nazi hands. The next day, on 16 May, the Germans outflanked the concrete and steel fortifications of the Maginot Line, built between 1930 and 1935 along France's border with Germany, and which

the French had believed to be impregnable. Churchill then learned that the French were to withdraw their forces altogether. Churchill responded with steadfast defiance and determination in a broadcast on 19 May. 'Is it not the appointed time for all to make the utmost exertions in their power?' he said. There now existed ' ... groups of shattered states and bludgeoned races: the Czechs, the Poles, the Norwegians, the Danes, the Dutch, the Belgians – upon all of whom the long night of barbarism will descend, unbroken even by a star of hope, unless we conquer, as conquer we must; as conquer we shall!'

GREAT DANGER

The retreat of the French forces had placed the British Expeditionary Force (BEF) in grave danger. These ten army divisions, which had crossed the Channel to reinforce the French in the first days of the war nine months earlier, were now directly in the path of the advancing German forces.

On 24 May, Churchill learned from the contents of captured documents that the Germans were planning to trap the BEF by cutting off their routes of retreat to the English Channel ports. That same night, he sent an urgent order for evacuation: the BEF were to head for the beaches and ports of Calais, Boulogne and Dunkirk along the north coast of France. The Royal Navy was ordered to prepare for an ambitious operation to rescue the men of the BEF and bring them home to England. But by 26 May, when the evacuation – codenamed Operation Dynamo – got under way, Dunkirk was the only port that had not yet been captured or which was not endangered by the rapidly encroaching German forces.

An emergency Cabinet meeting was held on 10 May, 1940 after the invasion of the Low Countries. Hours later, Chamberlain resigned in favour of Churchill, shown here with Ernest Bevin (left) and Anthony Eden (right). Bevin became Minister of Labour in the new government. Eden was reappointed Foreign Secretary.

CHURCHILL'S FIRST BROADCAST AS PRIME MINISTER, 19 MAY, 1940

I speak to you for the first time as Prime Minister in a solemn hour for the life of our country, of our Empire, of our Allies and above all, of the cause of freedom. A tremendous battle is raging in France and Flanders. The Germans, by a remarkable combination of air bombing and heavily armoured tanks, have broken through the French defences north of the Maginot Line and strong columns of their armoured vehicles are ravaging the open country .... They have penetrated deeply and spread alarm and confusion in their track. Behind them there are now appearing infantry in lorries and behind them, again, the large masses are moving forward .... We must not allow ourselves to be intimidated ... if the French retain that genius for recovery and counter-attack for which they have so long been famous; and if the British Army shows the dogged endurance and solid fighting power of which there have been so many examples in the past – then a sudden transformation of the scene might spring into being.

On 27 May, King Leopold III of Belgium asked the Germans for an armistice. This surrender meant that the men of the BEF were now in even greater danger: it removed the Belgian army from the path of the advancing Germans, opening up a dangerous gap on their eastern flank.

As May 1940 drew to a close, the evacuation at Dunkirk began. A mass of so-called 'little ships' – privately owned boats and yachts, paddle steamers and other pleasure craft from English coastal resorts – joined the Royal Navy in rescuing British and French soldiers from piers, jetties and a 10-mile stretch of beaches. Overhead, the German Luftwaffe pulverised the defensive perimeter around Dunkirk and blasted the rescue ships in the English Channel. The RAF claimed to have shot down 394 Luftwaffe planes for the loss of 114 of their own, but the prospects for the BEF remained grim.

Churchill leaves 10 Downing Street on 10 June, 1940, with his Parliamentary Private Secretary, Brendan Bracken. Clementine disliked Bracken, believing that he encouraged her husband's tendency to boastfulness and hasty judgment, but Bracken's unswerving support of Churchill helped him through his toughest times in office.

German tanks lined up around the perimeter were preparing to advance on Dunkirk when Hitler halted operations. The Führer's reasons for allowing the British and French to escape from Dunkirk have remained controversial ever since. His desire for a negotiated peace with Britain is an explanation often given; another is that his commanders were reluctant to risk their tanks in the difficult terrain around Dunkirk. What is certain is that the halt gave precious extra time to strengthen the perimeter, and enabled many

thousands of men to get away. By 4 June, when the rescue ended, an astonishing 338,226 British and French soldiers had been transported to England. Apart from 71 heavy artillery pieces and 595 vehicles, all their equipment had to be left behind. Yet it was, as Churchill called it, 'a miracle of deliverance'.

'NEVER SURRENDER'

Dunkirk was greeted in Britain as a triumph, and the men of the BEF came home to jubilant crowds. Churchill cautioned against the euphoria and in one of his most stirring speeches urged the nation to remain steadfast in their fight against tyranny. 'We must be careful not to assign to this deliverance the attributes of victory,' he warned the House of Commons on 4 June. 'Wars are not won by evacuations.' But he continued: 'Even though large tracts of Europe and many old and famous States have fallen or may fall into the grip of the Gestapo and all the odious apparatus of Nazi rule, we shall not flag or fail … We shall fight on the seas and oceans, we shall fight with growing confidence and growing strength in the air, we shall defend our island, whatever the cost may be. We shall fight on the beaches, we shall fight on the landing grounds, we shall fight in the fields and in the streets, we shall fight in the hills. We shall never surrender.'

On 26 June, 1940, Churchill stopped to greet two New Zealand soldiers who had recently arrived in Britain. Millions of troops from the dominions and colonies eventually joined in the war.

CHURCHILL BROADCASTS ON THE FRANCO-GERMAN ARMISTICE, 17 JUNE, 1940

The news from France is very bad and I grieve for the gallant French people who have fallen into this terrible misfortune. Nothing will alter our feelings towards them or our faith that the genius of France will rise again. What has happened in France makes no difference to our actions and purpose … we shall defend our island home and, with the British Empire, we shall fight on unconquerable until the curse of Hitler is lifted from the brows of mankind.

Although the United States was still unwilling to intervene, the events unfolding in Europe were beginning to impact upon them. Once the French surrendered, as seemed increasingly likely, the Germans would acquire new submarine bases along the western coast of France, which posed a great threat to Atlantic shipping. The 'battle of the Atlantic' was one of Churchill's greatest concerns. He called it 'the supreme menace of the War' for, if it were lost, the vital supply lines to Britain from America would be choked off, making defeat a certainty. The depredations of German surface raiders such as the pocket battleship *Admiral Graf Spee* and the battleship *Bismarck* made dramatic headlines but the major and continuing threat came from the German U-boats.

'How willingly I would have exchanged a full-scale invasion, for this shapeless, measureless peril,' Churchill wrote. 'This mortal danger to our lifeline gnawed at my bowels.'

BOOSTING MORALE

The threat to American shipping prompted the United States to ask for British help. The Americans wanted to lease bases in eight colonies of the British Empire in the Americas: Newfoundland, Bermuda, Trinidad, the Bahamas, Jamaica, Antigua, St Lucia and British Guiana. Churchill still lacked the 50 destroyers he wanted from the United States, and refused, but he sensed that here was some of the leverage he needed for his underlying goal: to circumvent the isolationists and persuade the United States to enter the war.

On 17 June, 1940, 11 days after the last soldiers were rescued from Dunkirk, the French asked the Germans for an armistice. The documents were signed on 22 June at Compiègne in France, the same location at which the 1918 armistice had been signed. France was divided between the German-controlled north and the remaining one-third of her territory governed by the collaborationist Vichy government headed by Marshal Philippe Pétain in the south. Britain was now alone in her defiance of Germany. There was renewed talk, especially abroad, that Britain would soon seek terms. It would require Churchill's most emphatic denials to dissipate these rumours. At the same time, national morale must be boosted and the British people fortified for the hard road ahead.

'The Battle of France is over,' Churchill had told the House of Commons on 18 June. 'I expect that the Battle of Britain is about to begin. Upon this battle depends the survival of Christian civilisation .... The whole fury and might of the enemy must very soon be turned on us. Hitler knows that he will have to break us in this island or lose the war. If we can stand up to him, all Europe may be free and the life of the world may move forward into broad, sunlit uplands. But if we fail, then the whole world, including the United States, including all that we have known and cared for, will sink into the abyss of a new Dark Age .... Let us therefore brace ourselves to our duties and so bear ourselves that if the British Empire and its Commonwealth last for a thousand years, men will still say "This was their finest hour."'

> 'Hitler knows that he will have to break us in this island or lose the war. If we can stand up to him, all Europe may be free and the life of the world may move forward into broad, sunlit uplands.'

Patriotic posters played an important role in keeping up morale during World War II. The slogan on this poster came from Churchill's 'blood, toil, tears and sweat' speech on 13 May, 1940: 'Come, then, let us go forward together with our united strength.'

"LET US
GO FORWARD
TOGETHER"

Churchill inspects the Scottish coastal defences in October 1940. The vulnerability of the defences had been highlighted a year earlier, when a U-boat sneaked into the Royal Navy base at Scapa Flow and sank the battleship Royal Oak.

and she tried to intervene. 'My darling', Clementine began, 'one of the men in your entourage – a devoted friend – has ... told me that there is a danger of your being generally disliked by your colleagues and subordinates because of your rough, sarcastic and overbearing manner .... My darling Winston, I must confess that I have noticed a deterioration in your manner and you are not so kind as you used to be ... I cannot bear that those who serve the country and yourself should not love you as well as admire and respect you. Besides, you won't get the best results by irascibility and rudeness ... '

A PAINFUL CHOICE

Churchill valued Clementine's advice, but had little time to adjust his conduct before he was faced with an agonising decision. It concerned the French fleet berthed at the naval base of Mers el Kebir, near Oran in Algeria. After the Franco-German Armistice was signed on 22 June, these powerful, well-equipped vessels were in danger of

falling into German hands. When the French authorities at Oran, who were loyal to the Vichy government, refused to co-operate with Britain by putting their ships out of reach, Churchill ordered the destruction of the fleet. On the morning of 3 July, 1940, the guns of Force H, the Royal Navy squadron in the Mediterranean, blew up one French cruiser, severely damaged another and killed 1300 French seamen. Churchill later wrote of this attack on a former ally as 'a hateful decision, the most unnatural and painful in which I have ever been concerned.'

The action at Mers el Kebir had unexpected, though salutary, effects. It removed any lingering doubts, especially in the United States, over

The Messerschmitt Bf 110 was used during the Battle of Britain to escort and protect German bombers. The twin-engined fighter was a disaster and had to be withdrawn because of its poor manoeuvrability and lack of speed, which made it vulnerable to the RAF's Spitfires and Hurricanes.

Britain's will to fight and win the war, and gave the British a new name for ruthless resolve. Churchill called Mers el Kebir 'the turning point in our fortunes. It made the world realise that we were in earnest in our intentions to carry on.'

RAF RESISTANCE

The next, more serious, test of Britain's will soon followed. Plans were being laid by the Germans for Operation Sealion, the invasion of Britain. In preparation for this, the Luftwaffe launched air attacks on Britain in order to destroy the RAF and establish supremacy of the air. The attacks began on 13 August – *Adlertag*, or Eagle Day. Field Marshal Hermann Goering, the head of the German air force, had every expectation of quick success. Aircraft production in Britain had accelerated since the war began, but not enough to confront Goering's Luftwaffe on equal terms. The RAF had only 650 Hurricane and Spitfire fighters to face the Luftwaffe's 2800 fighters, but this disparity was deceptive. The RAF managed to keep 600 Spitfires and Hurricanes in service every day, and these aircraft had the advantage of operating from their home bases. The equivalent figure for the Luftwaffe's Messerschmitt Bf 109s was 800, but their bases in the recently conquered territories of Belgium and France were not yet fully prepared. In addition, the Luftwaffe's flying time over

Britain was restricted to around 25 minutes by the limited amount of fuel their aircraft could carry.

But the most crucial advantage the RAF enjoyed was the chain of radar warning stations which could detect incoming raiders at long range. Radar enabled the RAF to concentrate its squadrons and have them waiting in the right place before the Luftwaffe arrived. August 1940 was hot and sunny. Day after day, the cloudless skies of southern England, scarred by the vapour trails of the contestants, afforded observers a grandstand view of the dogfights taking place overhead. The RAF made full use of the advantage of surprise radar allowed them. On 13 August the Luftwaffe flew 1485 sorties, yet failed to break the back of RAF resistance. German losses were three times greater – 45 aircraft shot down, compared to 13 RAF planes.

BRINK OF DEFEAT

Churchill had never lost his boyish sense of excitement at the prospect of history unfolding. News of how the aerial battle was progressing was brought to him at 10 Downing Street, the Prime Minister's official residence in London, but he wanted to witness the action for himself. On 15 August, he drove to Stanmore, north-west of London, to monitor the progress of the battle in the operations room of Fighter Command. The next day, he repeated the experience in the operations room of Fighter Command's 11 Group at Uxbridge in Middlesex.

The exploits of RAF pilots in the Battle of Britain, as it soon came to be known, assumed heroic proportions, and on 20 August, Churchill told the House of Commons: 'The gratitude of every home in our island, in our empire, and indeed throughout the world ... goes out to the British airmen who, undaunted by odds, unwearied in their constant challenge of mortal danger, are turning the tide of world war by their prowess and by their devotion. Never in the field of human conflict was so much owed by so many to so few.'

From 24 August, the Luftwaffe concentrated its attacks on airfields, aircraft factories, and communications and control centres, causing severe damage and putting many sector control stations out of action. By 5 September, the RAF had lost 450 aircraft, with 231 pilots killed or injured, and was on the brink of defeat. But total victory still eluded the Luftwaffe and, though critically damaged, the RAF was not ready to give up the fight.

From the start of the battle, Adolf Hitler and Hermann Goering had been looking for a single target whose destruction would achieve their ends quickly and decisively. Their first choice, the RAF, had proved tougher than expected, so they changed the focus of the attacks. On 7 September, 1940, they unleashed the fury of the Luftwaffe on London in the first of a long series of assaults that

'The gratitude of every home in our island, in our empire, and indeed throughout the world ... goes out to the British airmen who ... are turning the tide of world war by their prowess and by their devotion.'

CHURCHILL SPEAKING IN PARLIAMENT ON THE FIGHTING IN FRANCE 18 JUNE, 1940

The disastrous military events which have happened during the past fortnight have not come to me with any sense of surprise. Indeed, I indicated a fortnight ago as clearly as I could to the House that the worst possibilities were open; and I made it perfectly clear then that whatever happened in France would make no difference to the resolve of Britain and the British Empire to fight on, if necessary for years, if necessary alone.

The brave young pilots of the RAF, referred to as 'The Few' by Churchill, outmatched the German Luftwaffe in a fierce battle in the skies during the late summer of 1940. But casualties were high and the pilots had a life expectancy of just four to five weeks.

became known as the *blitz*. It was a tactical mistake, for it gave the RAF the time to recover their shattered airfields, which meant that British chances of survival improved. The blitz began with daylight raids, but the Luftwaffe lost too many bombers by day and later switched to night raids. During one attack, an air raid shelter took a direct hit, killing 40 people inside. Churchill came to survey the ruins and found himself surrounded by a crowd of survivors and bereaved relatives.

'We can take it! Give it 'em back!' they shouted, expressing their defiance with recently coined slogans. Churchill was so overwhelmed, he wept.

As the raids intensified, 10 Downing Street became vulnerable. On 16 September, Churchill, Clementine and the Downing Street staff moved into a specially fortified set of rooms in the Board of Trade Building opposite St James's Park. The rooms, which became known as the Number 10 Annexe, were strengthened inside by steel girders and outside by steel shutters. The shutters were closed as soon as the air raid siren sounded, in preparation for an impending attack. The annexe remained Churchill's headquarters for the rest of the war. In the underground basement, the Central War Rooms, later known as the Cabinet War Rooms, were built for

ON 10 SEPTEMBER, 1940, THREE DAYS INTO THE BLITZ ON LONDON, BATTERSEA WAS HIT BY A LUFTWAFFE AIR RAID ATTACK, WHICH DEVASTATED THE AREA. CHURCHILL VISITED THE SCENE TO SURVEY THE WRECKAGE AND MONITOR THE WORK OF THE AIR RAID WARDENS (WEARING STEEL HELMETS), WHOSE JOB IT WAS TO RESCUE PEOPLE TRAPPED UNDER THE DEBRIS.

meetings of Churchill's War Cabinet and the Defence Committee.

Churchill refused to remain inside his fortified bunker and spent nights watching from the roof of the government buildings in Whitehall – with searchlights scouring the skies overhead, the thunder of anti-aircraft guns and the whistle and roar of bombs descending and exploding. A year earlier, Churchill had believed that mercy should soften the brutalities of war – 'God forbid we should ever part company with that,' he had commented – but the sight of London ablaze around him hardened his heart. As his secretary John Colville noted in his diary on 19 September, the Prime Minister was 'becoming less and less benevolent towards the Germans ... and talks about castrating the lot!'

By the time the blitz ended in May 1941, the Luftwaffe had extended the bombing beyond London to Coventry, Liverpool and other industrial cities and ports. In just under nine months more than 43,000 civilians were killed,

Churchill (below) was appalled by the devastation caused by the blitz in December 1940. 'They burned a large part of the City of London ... ' he telegraphed Roosevelt, 'and the scenes of widespread destruction here ... are shocking.'

Churchill and Clementine (right) met General Wladyslaw Sikorski during a review of Polish troops in England. Sikorski was Prime Minister of the exiled Polish government based in London. The general was killed in a plane crash at Gibraltar in 1943.

another 51,000 were seriously injured and large areas of the bombed cities lay in ruins.

On 15 September, 1940, only eight days after the bombing of London began, the RAF brought an end to the Battle of Britain. That day, some 500 Luftwaffe aircraft crossed the English coast but only about 70 managed to reach their targets in central London. According to RAF statistics, 174 enemy aircraft were destroyed that day, and another nine were brought down by anti-aircraft fire. The British lost 25 aircraft and 13 pilots.

The same day, RAF bombers joined forces with Royal Navy ships to destroy some 200 barges moored along the coast of northern France, which were preparing for an invasion. Gradually the Luftwaffe's massed daylight raids tapered off. The

Churchill tries out a Sten 9mm sub-machine gun at a firing range in Kent early in 1941. Cheap, reliable and easy to produce in quantity, the Sten was widely used by British and Commonwealth forces during the war.

last of them took place on 30 September. The Germans had failed to take control of the air and without it, no invasion of England could succeed.

On 17 September, Hitler suspended Operation Sealion indefinitely. Britain was out of danger, but Churchill warned against a lapse in vigilance. 'Do not let us be lured into supposing that the danger is past,' he told the House of Commons. 'On the contrary, unwearying vigilance and the swift and steady strengthening of our Force by land, sea and air ... must be at all costs maintained .... Because we feel easier in ourselves and see our way more clearly through our difficulties and dangers than we did some months ago, because foreign countries, friends or foes, recognise the giant, enduring, resilient strength of Britain and the British Empire, do not let us dull for one moment the sense of the awful hazard in which we stand ... We must be united, we must be undaunted, we must be inflexible. Our qualities and deeds must burn and glow through the gloom of Europe until they become the veritable beacon of its salvation.'

BIRTH OF AN ALLIANCE

Churchill's dogged determination, together with the triumph of the Battle of Britain, combined to make a deep impression on President Roosevelt. He was now willing to make a deal with Churchill. In exchange for the bases the United States needed in the Caribbean, he agreed to supply the 50 American destroyers Churchill wanted to counteract the threat posed by German submarines. The Destroyers for Bases agreement was announced in September 1940. For Churchill, this was a significant achievement, as it symbolised the beginning of an alliance between Britain and the United States.

Roosevelt insisted on secrecy. Congress and the American nation as a whole were strongly opposed to intervening in Europe. A scheme for long-term cooperation was developed but given a cryptic name: the Standardisation of Arms Committee. Its purpose was to pinpoint and exploit strategic areas in which Britain and the United States could co-operate. Britain's most pressing needs were for food and armaments. When Harry Hopkins, Roosevelt's special envoy, arrived in Britain early in January 1941, he was informed that the US needed to send a minimum of 24 million tons of arms and 16 million tons of food to maintain the British war effort.

LEND-LEASE

Problems arose over how Britain was to pay for the war supplies. After only 15 months of war, Britain's gold and dollar reserves were seriously depleted: they totalled a little over half the cost of the arms supplies ordered for the first three months of 1941. Roosevelt solved the problem with the Lend-Lease arrangement, which allowed Britain to receive arms and other supplies from the United States and delay payment until after the war. Lend-Lease came with a hard bargain: Britain would have to pay some of her debts in gold and sell her commercial assets in the United States. Despite the harsh terms of the arrangement, it signalled to Churchill a long-term commitment to help Britain in the struggle against Hitler. The support of the United States was confirmed in talks held in Washington at the end of January 1941, which revealed that the Americans were willing to consider creating a unified military command for US and British forces, should the United States be forced into the war.

CHURCHILL BROADCASTS DURING THE BLITZ ON LONDON, 11 SEPTEMBER, 1940

These cruel, wanton, indiscriminate bombings of London are, of course, a part of Hitler's invasion plan. He hopes, by killing large numbers of civilians, and women and children, that he will terrorise and cow the people of this mighty ... city .... Little does he know the spirit of the British nation, or the tough fibre of the Londoners .... This wicked man, the repository and embodiment of many forms of soul-destroying hatreds ... has now resolved to try to break our famous island race .... What he has done is kindle a fire in British hearts ... which will glow long after all traces of the conflagration he has caused in London have been removed. He has lighted a fire which will burn with a steady and consuming flame until the last vestiges of Nazi tyranny have been burned out of Europe ....

On 10 May, 1940 an air raid attack destroyed the chamber of the House of Commons. 'The Huns obligingly chose a time when none of us was there,' Churchill told his son.

At the same time, Harry Hopkins concluded two more agreements with Churchill's government in London. First, where the need was urgent, American aircraft carriers would be made available to transport aircraft to Britain. Secondly, British and American intelligence in Nazi-occupied countries would pool their resources. Practical cooperation began before the end of January when a Purple encoding machine, the Japanese version of the German Enigma machine, arrived at the Government Code and Cipher School at Bletchley Park, Buckinghamshire, along with two American signals intelligence experts.

The Americans were keeping a careful watch on the Japanese, whose aggressions in China over the previous decade, coupled with their plans for economic dominance over the Pacific, looked as if they could escalate into war against the United States. Now the British were being allowed in on the act: with the Purple machine at their disposal, the decoding experts at Bletchley could read the thousands of top-secret radio signals sent out by Japanese diplomats, consular officials, naval and merchant ships.

Harry Hopkins returned to Washington at the end of January, impressed by what he had seen. Churchill had made sure that Roosevelt's emissary learned as much about Britain at war as he could manage during his busy three-week stay. Churchill took Hopkins to Scotland, where he heard the Prime Minister tell a Glasgow audience: 'My one aim is to extirpate Hitlerism from Europe'. The two men went to Dover where they surveyed the gun batteries pointing across the Channel towards the coast of Nazi-occupied France. While in London, Hopkins was able to observe how the life of the city and the good humour of Londoners were maintained, despite the air raids and rationing of food, clothing and fuel.

AMERICAN ADMIRATION

On his last weekend at Chequers before returning to the United States, Hopkins brought along a box of American gramophone records. Churchill took to the jazz, jive and Big Band tunes straight away, and the records were still playing at well past midnight. Churchill's Principal Private Secretary, Eric Seal, wrote that he had seen 'the PM walking about, sometimes dancing by himself in time to the music. We all got a bit sentimental and Anglo-American under the influence of a good dinner and the music.'

While he was in Britain, Hopkins formed a strong and enduring friendship with Churchill and

CHURCHILL ON THE GERMAN INVASION OF RUSSIA, 22 JUNE, 1941

At four o'clock this morning, Hitler attacked and invaded Russia. All his usual formalities of perfidy were observed with scrupulous technique. A non-aggression treaty had been solemnly signed and was in force between the two countries .... Under its cloak of false confidence, the German armies drew up in immense strength along the line which stretches from the White Sea to the Black Sea .... Then, suddenly, without declaration of war, without even an ultimatum, German bombs rained down from the air upon the Russian cities, the German troops violated the frontiers and an hour later, the German Ambassador, who till the night before was lavishing his assurances of friendship, almost of alliance, upon the Russians, called upon the Russian Foreign Minister to tell him that a state of war existed between Germany and Russia.

his admiration for the Prime Minister helped to break down the barriers that stood in the way of Anglo-American cooperation. 'He is the directing force behind the strategy and the conduct of the war in all its essentials,' Hopkins told President Roosevelt. 'He has an amazing hold on the British people of all classes and groups. He has particular strengths both with the military establishment and the working people.'

SPECIAL OPERATIONS

Churchill was impatient to get on with the action, and he was constantly throwing up new, often eccentric, ideas for pushing the war effort nearer to victory. One scheme was to seize territory in the north of Germany 'so that the enemy might be made to experience war in his own land'. Another of his ideas was to destabilise Nazi-occupied Europe by capturing Oslo, the Norwegian capital, so depriving Hitler of his 'first great achievement'. More feasible was Churchill's proposal for the Special Operations Executive. This clandestine organisation, better known as SOE, appealed to Churchill's sense of the unorthodox. Churchill established the organisation on 14 July, 1940, to coordinate the work of resistance groups within the occupied territories by supplying the secret agents, training and materials they needed for sabotage and subversion. Churchill described SOE as 'a new instrument of war' and one which, he predicted, would 'set Europe ablaze'. The phrase was flamboyant, but it proved an appropriate metaphor. In France, the main scene of SOE operations, the Resistance staged widespread disruption early on D-Day, 6 June, 1944, as a prelude to the Allied invasion of Normandy. Roads, railways, bridges and communications were sabotaged and German forces heading for the

Churchill described the Special Operations Executive as 'a new instrument of war' and one which, he predicted, would 'set Europe ablaze'. The phrase was flamboyant, but it proved ... appropriate....

beaches had to run a gauntlet of ambushes, where snipers felled soldiers and machine-gun nests left vehicles wrecked and burning.

In 1940 and the early months of 1941 the parameters of the war expanded. In North Africa, the British army became engaged in a struggle to prevent German forces and their Italian allies, who had declared war on 10 June, 1940, from seizing the vital Suez Canal in Egypt. In May 1941 the British liberated Ethiopia from more than five years of Italian occupation. Nearer home, Churchill and his Cabinet watched with concern a sinister pattern that was developing in south-east Europe.

On 9 January, 1941, Churchill received a decoded message revealing that the Luftwaffe was preparing for an invasion of Greece. An Italian invasion the previous October had gone badly and the Germans were stepping in to rescue their allies. In March 1939 Britain had promised to help the Greeks if they were attacked. Churchill and his War Cabinet were anxious to make good the promise, but there were difficulties. In North Africa, the German Afrika Korps, led by General Erwin Rommel, was achieving spectacular success in the Western Desert. Withdrawing men and supplies for Greece could compromise British efforts to safeguard Egypt and the Suez Canal.

GREECE AND THE BALKANS

Churchill was cautious. 'Do not consider yourself obligated to the Greek enterprise, if in your hearts you feel it will be another Norwegian fiasco,' he told Anthony Eden and General Archibald Wavell, Commander-in-Chief of British forces in the Middle East. 'If no good plan can be made, please say so. But of course,' Churchill added slyly, 'you know how valuable success would be.' As he had hoped, plans to send aid to Greece went ahead. Meanwhile, a pro-Nazi bloc was taking shape in south-east Europe. Hungary and Romania allied themselves to Nazi Germany in 1940 and Bulgaria was soon to follow. Yugoslavia completed the quartet on 24 March, 1941 when Dr Dragisha Cvetkovic, its pro-Nazi Prime Minister, signed a treaty with Hitler. The treaty was repudiated two days later when royalist insurgents overthrew Cvetkovic. Hitler, enraged, gave orders that the Yugoslavs should be brought to heel 'with merciless brutality'. The German forces saw to it that his orders were carried out, and on 17 April, after eleven days' resistance, the Yugoslav Army surrendered. Their brief struggle had cost them 90,000 prisoners, the deaths of thousands of civilians and the almost complete devastation of their capital, Belgrade.

The Greeks suffered a similar fate. On 6 April the Luftwaffe struck the Greek port of Piraeus,

where British military supplies were being unloaded: six ships were sunk and another, loaded with 200 tons of high explosives, blew up at its moorings. Piraeus was devastated. Elsewhere, the German forces moved swiftly through the Greek defence lines, capturing Salonika on 9 April and forcing the withdrawal of the Greek 1st Army and its surrender on 21 April.

The British forces in Greece were now in a desperate position. Some 75,000 men under the command of General Henry Maitland Wilson were obliged to make a rapid retreat. Plans were

Churchill had an entourage of secret agents during his visit to Washington DC on 26 December, 1941, when he addressed both houses of Congress for the first time. That night, the enormous emotional strain and great physical exertions of two years of war leadership caught up with Churchill and he suffered his first heart attack. Fortunately it was mild.

Patriotic 'Fight for Freedom' posters featuring Churchill appeared in 1941. The inscription 'Give us the tools and we will finish the job' came from a broadcast Churchill made in London on 9 February, 1941. The message was addressed to the Americans who were sending vital war supplies to Britain, although they were not yet combatants in the war.

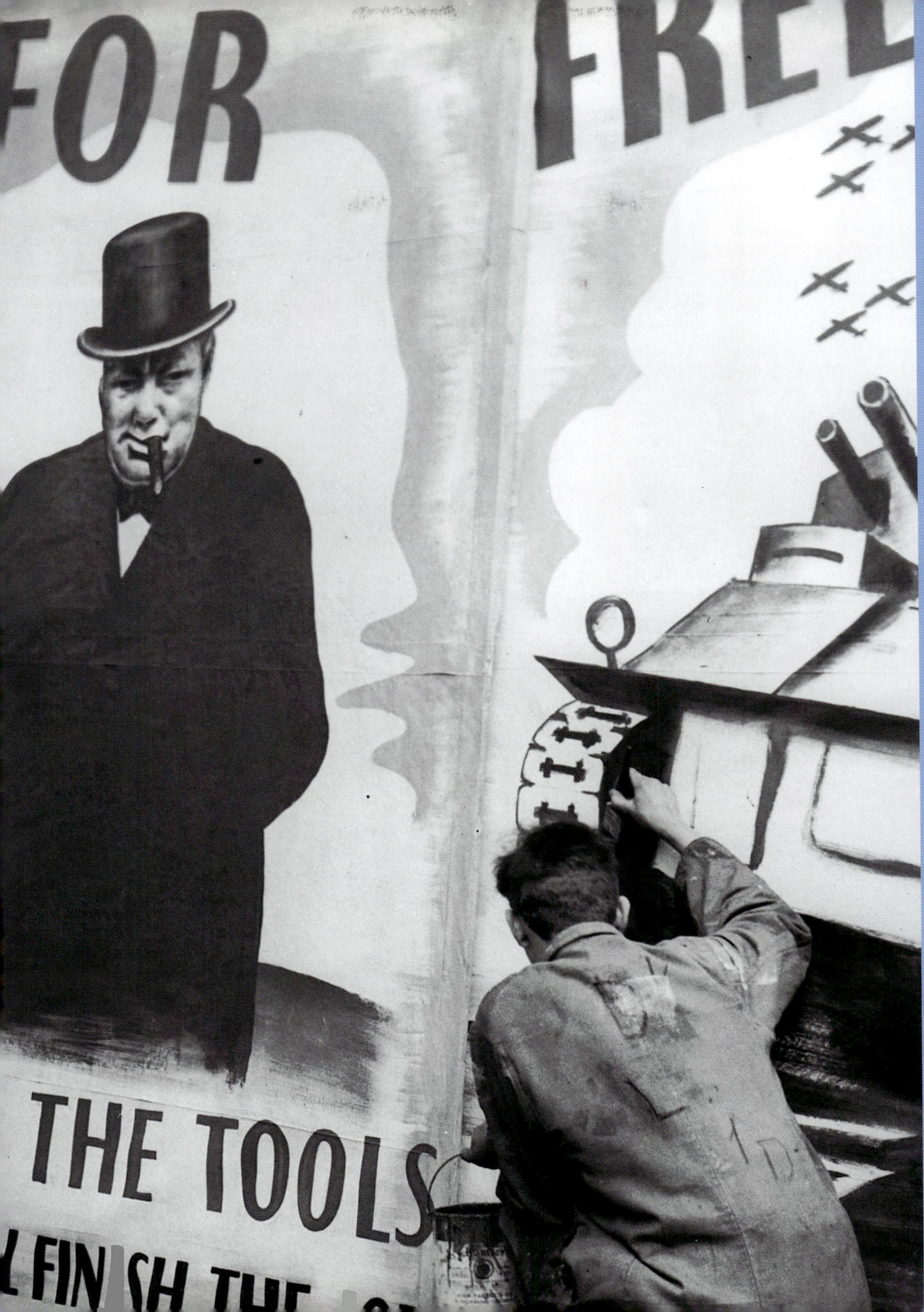
FOR
THE TOOLS

During his visit to North America in 1941, Churchill addressed a joint session of the Canadian Parliament in Ottawa on 30 December. In his speech, Churchill referred to the gloomy predictions made by French generals in 1940 that 'In three weeks, England will have her neck wrung like a chicken!' To this he retorted: 'Some chicken! Some neck!'

laid to evacuate the troops to the island of Crete – a British base since 1940. But the Luftwaffe prevented the troops from making an easy getaway. Stukas, the much-feared German war planes, dive-bombed and machine-gunned the transports for a week, killing thousands of men. In all, 50,000 troops were evacuated to Crete.

FACADE OF CONFIDENCE

The Germans followed them in overwhelming numbers, landing a total of 22,000 troops on the island after 20 May. The exhausted, ill-equipped defenders held out for more than a week until the Royal Navy arrived to evacuate them. In the process, the navy lost more than 2000 men, and 5000 soldiers had to surrender to the Germans.

The disastrous seven-week campaign in Greece and Crete badly damaged British morale and prestige. Then came further bad news from North Africa, where the lightning German advance of Rommel's Afrika Korps had pushed British forces back across the desert to the Egyptian frontier.

Churchill put an optimistic interpretation on the downturn in British fortunes. Broadcasting from Chequers, he reassured the nation of ultimate victory. 'No prudent and far-seeing man can doubt that the eventual and total defeat of Hitler and Mussolini is certain, in view of the respective resolves of the British and American democracies.'

Beneath the façade of confidence, Churchill was on edge. On 27 April, when Major-General John Kennedy, Director of Military Operations at the War Office, suggested over dinner at Chequers that the British Army might have to evacuate Egypt, Churchill became so incensed that his other guests had difficulty calming him down. Ten days later Churchill's mood darkened further when he was criticised in the Commons over Egypt, the fiasco in Greece and Crete, and German successes in the vital Battle of the Atlantic. In the three months from March to June 1941, by Luftwaffe air action alone, 167,000 tons of shipping per month were being sunk. Churchill demanded a vote of confidence. He won it by 447 votes for, to three against. It was a decisive margin, but the experience was unsettling.

In the summer of 1941, Churchill was distracted from criticism at home by a new development: the Russo-German non-aggression pact, signed in 1939, was about to be torn up. For some time, the Germans had been massing troops, tanks and armament on their border with Russia.

Now, the alliances in the Balkans and the conquests of Greece and Yugoslavia came into focus: the Germans had been protecting their southern flank as a prelude to their invasion of Russia.

At 4:00AM on 22 June, 1941, around 150 German divisions crossed into Russian territory along a line stretching nearly 1250 miles northwards from the Black Sea to the Arctic Circle. Britain was no longer fighting alone. Yet, if the Soviets lost, as Churchill believed they would, it could give Hitler the chance to concentrate the whole military might of Germany on another invasion of Britain.

Luftwaffe bombers dropped 503 tons of high explosives and 881 incendiary canisters on Coventry during a ten-hour raid on 14 November, 1940, devastating St Michael's Cathedral and the area around it.

TOTAL WAR

In 1941, Britain was joined by two allies: Soviet Russia, invaded by the Nazis in June, and the USA, which declared war after the Japanese attacked Pearl Harbor on 7 December. The next day, Churchill kept a promise made to Roosevelt in November and declared war on Japan. After initial setbacks, the tide slowly began to turn in the Allies' favour.

The Nazi invasion of Russia forced Churchill out of a mindset that he had held for almost a quarter of a century. He saw at once the need to set aside his hatred of Communism and give all possible support to the Soviets as the most recent victims of Nazi aggression. In a radio broadcast on 22 June, 1941, Churchill acknowledged that no-one had been a more consistent opponent of Communism than him, but added that ' ... all this fades away before the spectacle which is now unfolding. The past, with its crimes, its follies, its tragedies, flashes away ... we shall give whatever help we can to Russia and the Russian people ... The Russian danger is ... our danger.'

Churchill was already passing on decrypted German radio messages to Josef Stalin, the Soviet leader, ten days before the Nazi invasion took place. Churchill was careful to keep from him the source of the intelligence – the Bletchley Park code-breaking machine. Five days after the start of the invasion, Bletchley Park broke the Enigma key the Germans were using in Russia and again passed decrypts to Stalin, enabling Red Army commanders to anticipate German strategy. Churchill at once ordered diversionary attacks to distract the invaders from their Russian campaign. Only

Speaking on 14 July, 1941, Churchill (left) praised the grit of Londoners as they confronted the depredations of the blitz. 'You do your worst – and we will do our best.' Churchill (above) returns from his historic meeting with President Roosevelt at Placentia Bay, Newfoundland.

William Lyon Mackenzie King, Prime Minister of Canada, visited Churchill at Downing Street on 21 August, 1941. Canada declared war on Germany on 10 September, 1939, and by 1945 more than 1,300,000 Canadians had served in World War II.

two days after the invasion he sanctioned the bombing of German military and naval installations in northern France, and ten days later initiated a series of night raids against the Rhineland and Germany's main industrial area, the Ruhr. On 6 July, the RAF flew 400 sorties over northern France and that night, Germany was attacked again by a force of 250 bombers. By 12 July, the joint war aims of Britain and the Soviet Union were formalised by an agreement of mutual assistance, signed in Moscow. 'We shall do everything to help you that time, geography and our growing resources allow,' Churchill told Stalin by telegram on 7 July. 'We have only to go on fighting to beat the life out of these villains.'

The Prime Minister showed a confident façade to Stalin and the world, but behind it, he feared the Soviets would be defeated. Despite his warnings to Stalin, the Soviet leader had not expected the invasion to come and the Red Army was unprepared. More than 600,000 Soviet troops were taken prisoner, and the remainder

retreated rapidly before the German *blitzkrieg*. The Germans made rapid progress and were within 224 miles of Moscow in four weeks. Churchill was not alone in doubting the Soviets' prospects. Churchill's Foreign Minister, Anthony Eden, as well as the British Ambassador to Moscow, Sir Stafford Cripps, and Sir John Dill, Chief of the General Staff, were also convinced their resistance could not last. The US Ambassador in Britain, John Gilbert Winant, gave the Soviets a mere six weeks before they would fall to the Nazi forces.

Six weeks passed and the Soviets were still holding out, but the supplies Churchill had sent to Russia were beginning to deplete Britain's own stocks and, crucially, to reduce the number of fighter aircraft at the disposal of the RAF. The Americans, Churchill decided, would have to provide matériel Britain was unable to furnish.

PLACENTIA BAY TALKS

In August 1941 Churchill crossed the Atlantic bound for Newfoundland in eastern Canada, where he met the American President at Placentia Bay. It was not their first encounter. They had met briefly at the end of World War I. Churchill had been impressed by Roosevelt then, but now admired him even more for his strength of will and determination, which had enabled him to fight his way back into politics and to the presidency after being crippled by polio at the age of 39. 'I have established warm and deep personal relations with our great friend,' Churchill later told the War Cabinet.

Before talks began in earnest, Churchill and some of his entourage disembarked for an afternoon to explore the shoreline at Placentia Bay. According to one member of his staff, Colonel Ian Jacob, they 'clambered over some rocks and the PM like a schoolboy, (got) a great kick out of rolling boulders down a cliff.' Talks began on 11 August and at first Churchill was pleased with the results. The discussions produced an impressive statement of democratic intent in a document later known as the Atlantic Charter. Among its provisions, Britain and the United States pledged to protect the right of peoples to choose their own governments and to live free

Churchill sailed to Placentia Bay, Newfoundland, on board HMS Prince of Wales *in August 1941. Four months later, he was distressed to learn that the battleship had been sunk in the Pacific by the Japanese.*

from fear. Roosevelt also promised to commit the United States to even greater involvement in the war, including supplying aid to the Soviet Union 'on a gigantic scale', more merchant ships to transport tanks and bombers to Britain, and five destroyers for each convoy sailing the dangerous North Atlantic run.

But it soon became clear that the Americans were no closer to joining the war: when Roosevelt returned to Washington he assured the American people that Placentia Bay had produced no commitment to enter the conflict. What was needed, Roosevelt confided to Churchill, was a big, dramatic incident that would instantly clear

away all doubts and propel the United States to war on a wave of national outrage.

In a telegram, Churchill told his friend Harry Hopkins: 'There has been a wave of depression through Cabinet and other informed circles here (over) the President's many assurances about no commitments and no closer to war etc.' Churchill's main concern was that a German victory in Russia would have dire consequences for Britain. 'If Germany beat Russia to a standstill, and the United States made no further advance towards entry into the war, there was a great danger that the war might take a turn against us.'

RAYS OF HOPE

In September 1941, this outcome seemed imminent. The Germans were closing in on Moscow. In the north, they were besieging Leningrad. In the south, they captured Kiev in the Ukraine. The Caucasus and its valuable oil wells were almost within reach. Stalin grew increasingly agitated. Churchill sought to assuage the Soviet leader's fears with a generous aid package. He promised to send Russia half the aircraft and tanks Stalin had requested and urged the Americans to provide the rest.

A joint British and Soviet force occupied oil-rich Iran to create a northward route for oil supplies to Russia. Another route, to Murmansk, the only major ice-free port in northern Russia, was opened up in September. Despite terrible, freezing conditions and fierce attacks by German submarines and aircraft, Britain shipped 4 million tonnes of war matériel and other supplies to the hard-pressed Soviets via Murmansk. Churchill reassured Stalin: 'We shall batter Germany from the air with unceasing severity and keep the seas open and ourselves alive.'

On 29 August, 1941, representatives of all the Allied governments were invited to the Soviet embassy in London. It was an extraordinary, but cordial, meeting of ideological foes, who set aside their differences to confront the common German enemy.

CHURCHILL BROADCASTS TO THE NAZI-OCCUPIED COUNTRIES OF EUROPE, 24 AUGUST, 1941

The ordeals ... of conquered peoples will be hard. We must give them hope; we must give them the conviction that their sufferings and their resistances will not be in vain .... Do not despair, brave Norwegians; your land shall be cleansed ... from the invader .... Be sure of yourselves, Czechs: your independence shall be restored. Poles, the heroism of your people ... shall not be forgotten; your country shall live again .... Tough, stout-hearted Dutch, Belgians, Luxembourgers, tormented, mishandled, shamefully cast away people of Yugoslavia ... yield not an inch! Keep your souls clean from all contact with the Nazis; make them feel ... that they are the moral outcasts of mankind. Help is coming; mighty forces are arming on your behalf. Have faith. Have hope, deliverance is sure!

Fortunately, Bletchley Park decrypts were able to provide some hope. In September and October, Churchill learned that Luftwaffe units in Russia were suffering major supply and maintenance problems. It was too late in the year for the quick *blitzkrieg* victory Hitler had anticipated and as the Russian winter advanced, German prospects worsened.

Meanwhile Churchill's restless imagination searched for any possible opportunities for action. In late October 1941 he produced plans for two amphibious assaults, one against occupied Norway, the other against the Mediterranean island of Sicily, to help the forthcoming British offensive against Rommel's Afrika Korps in North Africa. To Churchill's disappointment, the Chiefs of Staff turned down both proposals, considering them to be too risky and impractical. Under War Cabinet rules, the Prime Minister had no powers to override their decisions and he became frustrated at what he considered their lack of daring. 'The Admirals, Generals and Air Marshals chant their stately hymn of "Safety First",'

During his trip to the USA and Canada at the end of 1941, Churchill visited a Canadian Air Force School at Upland Airport in Ottawa, accompanied by C G Powers, the Canadian Air Minister for National Defence (left) and Wing Commander William MacBrien (centre). During the war, Canada hosted the Empire Air Training Scheme set up in November 1939 to provide pilots for the Royal Air Force.

In the surprise Japanese air raid on Pearl Harbor, the damage to US aircraft was exacerbated by the fact that they were parked wingtip-to-wingtip as a defence against sabotage.

friendship for Ronnie and Victor, the companions of gay subaltern days and early wars, is a personal bond between us, to which will soon be added the comradeship of action in fateful events.'

GLOBAL WAR

Unknown to Churchill, a fateful event was only three weeks away. On 7 December, 1941, without any warning or declaration of war, Japanese carrier-borne aircraft attacked the US Pacific fleet at anchor in the American naval base at Pearl Harbor, Hawaii. By the time the two-hour assault ended the Americans, caught unawares, had lost 5 warships, 187 aircraft and some 2400 personnel. On what he later termed 'a day that will live in infamy', President Roosevelt had at last found the justification he had been seeking and on 8 December Congress declared war. When Churchill telephoned for news Roosevelt told him: 'We are all in the same boat now.'

Immediately after the attack on Pearl Harbor, which was designed to prevent the US from interfering with Japan's expansionist plans in the Pacific, a Japanese tide of conquest swept across the ocean, engulfing American territories and colonies of the British, French and Dutch empires one after the other. Nazi Germany and Italy, Japan's partners in the Axis Tripartite Pact signed in September 1940, declared war on the United States on 11 December. Churchill was both saddened and relieved. 'We must expect to suffer heavily in this war with Japan,' he wrote to Clementine. ' ... The entry of the United States into the war is worth all the losses sustained in

Churchill wrote to his son, Randolph. 'I have to restrain my natural pugnacity by sitting on my own head!'

Churchill longed for a tough-minded companion who would share his urge to go on the offensive and strike the enemy with maximum force. His impetuous nature meant he often clashed with his cautious Chief of Imperial General Staff, (CIGS), General Sir John Dill. Churchill eventually lost patience and dismissed Dill, replacing him with General Alan Brooke on 16 November. There was a personal tie between Churchill and his new CIGS. In his youth, Churchill had been friends with Brooke's two brothers, Victor and Ronald, both of them now dead. Churchill wrote to Brooke on 18 November. 'I feel that my old

the East many times over. Still, these losses are very painful to endure and will be very hard to repair.'

December's declarations of war prompted Roosevelt to ask for another meeting with Churchill. The Prime Minister arrived in Washington after a ten-day transatlantic journey, and was the President's guest at the White House for the next three weeks. The Prime Minister was tired of defensive actions and longed to take the initiative with a landing in enemy-occupied

On 26 December, 1941, two weeks after the United States entered the war, Churchill addressed a joint session of Congress in Washington: 'As long as we have faith in our cause and an unconquerable willpower, salvation will not be denied us.'

territory. The talks with Roosevelt produced agreement on this score, though the landing place was not in Europe, but North Africa, where an Anglo-American force could expect to make relatively easy progress against the Vichy French defenders. After some tough negotiation, the American Chiefs of Staff agreed that Europe, rather than Asia, would be the primary theatre of war.

Four days later, on 26 December, Churchill suffered a mild heart attack while struggling to open a window in his overheated room. The standard treatment was at least six weeks in bed, but Churchill's doctor, Charles Wilson, later Lord Moran, realised this was impossible. As one of the major war leaders, the Prime Minister could not be revealed to the world as an invalid with a bad heart. Wilson took a big risk. He kept his diagnosis to himself, and did not even tell Churchill. Instead,

he informed him that he was suffering from a sluggish circulation and recommended no undue exertion.

A CLOSE SHAVE

Though tired and weak, Churchill managed to continue talks with the Americans. It appears nobody suspected anything was wrong, although he did take a week's break at a beach-side bungalow in Miami before the conference ended on 12 January, 1942.

Churchill started his return journey to Britain by flying to Bermuda, from where he was due to board ship for his passage home. During the flight, Churchill's fascination with aircraft surfaced and he asked if he could take the controls. He flew the plane for 20 minutes, making two banking turns before handing the controls back to the pilot, who was impressed with his performance.

Bad news awaited Churchill in Bermuda. Singapore, in the British colony of Malaya, was in imminent danger of falling to the Japanese. Churchill cancelled the sea voyage home and opted instead to return by flying boat, which

'I want to make it absolutely clear that I expect every inch of ground to be defended, every scrap of material or defences to be blown to pieces to prevent capture by the enemy and no question of surrender to be entertained ... '

could cover the 3365 miles to Britain in less than 18 hours. The change of plan nearly ended in disaster. The flying boat was off course as it approached Plymouth on the south coast of England, and was veering towards the target zone of German anti-aircraft guns sited at Brest on the Atlantic coast of Brittany in France. The error was corrected and the flying boat altered course northward, but coming from that direction, it was identified by radar at Plymouth as a 'hostile bomber'. Sector controllers issued orders for fighters to intercept the intruder and Churchill was within minutes of being shot down when the mistake was, fortunately, discovered.

The news from south-east Asia that had brought Churchill hurrying home was grim. The garrison at Singapore was on the brink of being overrun, and surrender seemed imminent. Churchill refused to countenance it. 'I want to make it absolutely clear,' he telegraphed to Field Marshal Sir Archibald Wavell, British Supreme Commander Far East, on 20 January, 'that I

CHURCHILL REFUSES TO NEGOTIATE PEACE WITH GERMANY, 9 SEPTEMBER, 1941

We are told ... that we must soon expect what is called a 'peace offensive' from Berlin .... They ... show that the guilty men who have let Hell loose upon the world are hoping to escape, with their fleeting triumphs and ill-gotten plunders, from the closing net of doom. We owe it to ourselves, we owe it to our Russian ally and to the government and people of the United States, to make it absolutely clear that whether we are supported or alone, however long and hard the toil may be, the British nation and His Majesty's government in intimate concert with the governments of the great Dominions will never enter into any negotiations with Hitler or any party in Germany which represents the Nazi regime.

Churchill (third from left) joined President Roosevelt (on his left) and Mrs Eleanor Roosevelt (on his right) to attend a Christmas service in Washington in 1941. Though his legs were paralysed by polio, the President was able to stand with the support of metal callipers.

expect every inch of ground to be defended, every scrap of material or defences to be blown to pieces to prevent capture by the enemy, and no question of surrender to be entertained until after protracted fighting among the ruins of Singapore City.' Churchill had already told his Chiefs of Staff that 'commanders, staffs and principal officers are expected to perish at their posts'.

'THE GREATEST DISASTER'

The news got worse. Despite Churchill's strictures, General Arthur Percival, in command at Singapore, surrendered to the Japanese on 15 February, 1942 and 62,000 British, Australian and Indian soldiers were taken prisoner. The loss of Singapore hit Churchill hard. He called it 'the greatest disaster to British arms which our history records'. He had not fully recovered from his heart attack in Washington, yet still put on a pugnacious, optimistic front to the world. The strain was immense. As Captain Richard Pim, head of Churchill's War Map Room, noted on 18 February, 1942: 'He said he was tired of it all; he is very seriously thinking of handing over his responsibilities to other shoulders.'

Churchill's black mood was only a temporary lapse. On 24 February, when he was pressured in Parliament to relinquish his second role as Minister of Defence, Churchill was ready with a typically vigorous answer. He told the Commons: 'However tempting it may be to some, when much trouble lies ahead, to step aside adroitly and put someone else up to take the blows, the heavy and repeated blows, which are coming, I do not intend to adopt that cowardly course.'

CHURCHILL CAUSED MUCH INTEREST IN THE UNITED STATES WHEN HE APPEARED BEFORE PRESS CAMERAS IN WASHINGTON WEARING HIS 'SIREN' SUIT, SO-CALLED BECAUSE THE ZIPPED, ONE-PIECE GARMENT HAD BEEN SPECIALLY DESIGNED TO LET HIM DRESS WITHIN A MINUTE AT THE SOUND OF AN AIR-RAID SIREN IN THE MIDDLE OF THE NIGHT.

Churchill is pictured here with his daughter Mary on 2 July, 1942, the day he was confronted with a vote of censure against him in the House of Commons over his conduct of the war. Only 25 MPs supported the motion.

Churchill faced more pressing challenges than those in Parliament. Stalin was urging his allies to make an Anglo-American landing in northern Europe, to create a second front that would relieve the pressure on Soviet forces. But despite their enormous industrial capacity, the Americans were not yet ready to comply, and in 1942 could provide only 40 per cent of the men and matériel required. The only alternative capable of sapping German strength and willpower was the continued bombing of German cities. Churchill had no faith that bombing would prove a decisive factor in the war, but the campaign escalated after the first thousand bomber raid struck Cologne at the end of May 1942. Though enormously destructive on the ground, the raids were costly in bombers and aircrew lives. After three more mass raids, casualties were so great that thousand bomber attacks were halted and not resumed until 1944.

In the third week of June Churchill flew to the United States for another meeting with the President at the Roosevelt mansion in Hyde Park, New York. Roosevelt personally drove Churchill to his splendid home and impressed the Prime Minister with the deft way he used the special controls on his car. 'Mr Roosevelt's infirmity prevented him from using his feet on the brake, clutch or accelerator,' Churchill wrote later. 'An ingenious arrangement enabled him to do everything with his arms, which were amazingly strong and muscular. This was reassuring.' It was a hair-raising journey at times. Churchill continued '…but I confess that when on several occasions, the car poised and backed on the grass verges of the precipices over

Churchill takes a trip along the River Thames on 25 July, 1942 with several US diplomats, including John Gilbert Winant, US ambassador to Britain (third from left), with whom he was dining when he received news of the Japanese attack at Pearl Harbor. Churchill had been so incensed that he wanted to instruct the Foreign Office to declare war on Japan immediately.

the Hudson (River), I hoped the mechanical devices and brakes would show no defects.'

CRITICISMS AT HOME

The talks at Hyde Park were productive and included a secret agreement that Britain and the United States would share research into the creation and manufacture of an atomic bomb. They also gave the go-ahead for an Anglo-American amphibious landing in one of the Vichy-ruled French possessions along the North African coast. Churchill remained in America for five days before returning home to what he told his friend Harry Hopkins promised to be 'a beautiful row'. On 2 July, a Liberal MP, Leslie Hore-Belisha, launched a fierce attack on the way the war had been handled leading to a Vote of Censure in the House of Commons. 'In a hundred days,' Hore-Belisha declared, 'we have lost our Empire in the Far East. What will happen in the next hundred days?'

Another critic, the Labour MP Aneurin Bevan, was more personal. 'The Prime Minister wins

On Churchill's visit to the United States in June 1942, he was taken to Fort Jackson in South Carolina to watch a demonstration of US Army parachute troop techniques.

debate after debate and loses battle after battle,' he complained. 'The country is beginning to say that he fights debates like a war and the war like a debate.' It hardly helped Churchill's case that eleven days before the debate took place, Rommel's Afrika Korps had succeeded in capturing Tobruk in Libya from the British garrison, putting the Germans in a position to threaten Cairo, the capital of Egypt. Churchill launched a robust defence of his government's record, telling the House: 'If those who have assailed us are reduced to contemptible proportions and their Vote of Censure on the National Government is converted to a vote of censure upon its authors, make no mistake – a cheer will go up from every friend of Britain and

CHURCHILL SALUTES THE ENTRY OF THE UNITED STATES INTO THE WAR, 26 DECEMBER, 1941

Five or six years ago, it would have been easy, without shedding a drop of blood, for the United States and Great Britain to have insisted on fulfilment of the disarmament clauses of the treaties which Germany signed after the Great (First World) War …. That chance has passed. It is gone. Prodigious hammer strokes have been needed to bring us together again … some great purpose and design is being worked out here below, of which we have the honour to be faithful servants …. I avow my hope and faith, sure and inviolate, that in the days to come the British and American peoples will for their own safety and for the good of all walk together side by side in majesty, in justice and in peace.

every faithful servant of our cause, and the knell of disappointment will ring in the ears of the tyrants we are striving to overthrow.'

The Censure motion was easily quashed – with a mere 25 voting in favour to 475 against. But in mid July Churchill received more bad news: a large convoy, code-named PQ17, had been devastated on the Arctic run to Murmansk by German U-boats and torpedo bombers, which sank 24 of its 35 ships. The attacks brought the total losses of the Arctic convoys to 60 ships sunk in 1942. The death toll was immense and the convoys for August and September were cancelled. The attacks also

ruled out the possibility of an Anglo-American landing to open up a 'second front' in northern Europe. Stalin was infuriated, not least because the Germans had recently broken through the Caucasus defences in southern Russia and were heading for the precious oil wells.

On 12 August Churchill flew to Moscow from Cairo to meet face-to-face with Stalin. He made

Churchill takes a closer look at the paratroopers during his visit to Fort Jackson. During World War II, airborne troops represented a new means of invasion and attack, both in Europe and the Pacific.

the ten-and-a-half hour flight in the unpressurised cabin of an American *Liberator* bomber, wearing an oxygen mask specially adapted so that he could smoke his cigar. In Moscow, Churchill found Stalin volatile, veering between anger and despondency. Churchill was careful to keep his temper and his tough, retributive talk thawed Stalin's hostility. The Soviet leader was cheered by the Prime Minister's promise that air raids would 'shatter almost every dwelling in almost every German city'.

'(This) had a very stimulating effect upon the meeting,' Churchill later recalled, 'and thenceforward, the atmosphere became progressively more cordial.' Churchill's five-day visit ended with a banquet hosted by Stalin. It had been a nervy experience, but the meeting brought an important benefit: the Soviet leader agreed to

'I have never promised anything but blood, tears, toil and sweat. Now, however, we have a new experience. We have victory, a remarkable and definite victory.'

provide long-range air cover for the reinstated September convoy to Murmansk. This, together with a powerful destroyer escort, ensured that when the convoy sailed on 14 September the number of ships sunk was reduced by almost a third.

By the autumn of 1942 Churchill saw the first glimmer of victory on the horizon. On 23 October, a tremendous artillery barrage flashed across the night sky over the desert near El Alamein, an Egyptian town some 50 miles west of Alexandria. It was the prelude to an advance by the British Eighth Army, which was moving inexorably towards the defence lines of Rommel's Afrika Korps. By 4 November the Afrika Korps was in full retreat westwards. Churchill ordered church bells to be rung all over Britain to acknowledge the victory. On 8 November, Anglo-American troops landed

In August 1942, Churchill toured 8th Army defences in the Western Desert, which, according to decrypted German messages, were to be the targets of Afrika Korps assaults in the coming offensive.

along the Algerian coast of North Africa in Operation Torch. Algiers, the capital of the French colony of Algeria, surrendered on 10 November and a ceasefire was arranged with the Vichy French forces the next day.

THE TIDE BEGINS TO TURN

In London, Churchill spoke of the triumph at El Alamein at the Lord Mayor's Luncheon at the Mansion House. 'I have never promised anything but blood, tears, toil and sweat,' he said. 'Now, however, we have a new experience. We have victory, a remarkable and definite victory. The bright gleam has caught the helmets of our soldiers, and warmed and cheered all our hearts.'

Neither El Alamein nor Operation Torch were isolated triumphs. They were only two in a series of hard-won successes that turned the gloom of 1940-1941 into fresh hope for the future. In June 1942, off Midway Island in the north Pacific Ocean, the Americans defeated the Japanese in the first sea battle fought exclusively between naval air forces. Four Japanese aircraft carriers were sunk – half their entire carrier force. It was a critical loss from which the Japanese Imperial Navy never fully recovered.

By the end of 1942 the British and Americans were at last getting the better of the German U-boats in the Battle of the Atlantic. Faster convoy escorts had now been introduced. Hunter-killer convoy support groups were formed, comprising ships and aircraft dedicated to the detection, pursuit and destruction of German submarines. Aircraft such as Liberator bombers were equipped for the purpose with the latest high-detection radar, airborne searchlights, machine-guns and depth charges.

At the end of January 1943 the remnants of the German 6th Army surrendered to the Soviets at Stalingrad after five months of savage warfare fought in atrocious winter conditions. From then on, the Germans, like the Japanese, were never able to regain the upper hand. The tide of war had finally turned.

Churchill met British Service Chiefs and members of the Middle East War Council at the British Embassy in Cairo during his visit to Egypt and the Western Desert in 1942.

TOWARDS OPERATION OVERLORD

In 1943, the fighting in North Africa ended and both Sicily and mainland Italy were invaded by the Allies, forcing a surrender. Churchill and Roosevelt, later joined by Stalin, met in a series of conferences to plan the final downfall of Nazi Germany, which began with the invasion of Normandy on D-Day, 6 June, 1944.

Even before the United States entered World War II at the end of 1941, Churchill had eagerly awaited an Allied invasion of Adolf Hitler's 'Fortress Europe'. On a clear day the most likely point of attack, the coast of northern France, was visible across the English Channel. It was temptingly close, but lack of manpower, weaponry and transport put it out of reach. The Americans had begun to mobilise troops but they were nowhere near ready for an assault on this scale. When Churchill and Roosevelt met at Hyde Park on 20 June, 1942, they agreed that there were too few US combat aircraft or landing craft available for the cross-Channel invasion to go ahead in early 1943, as they had originally hoped.

Despite this agreement, Roosevelt wanted to make a landing on the Cherbourg coast of France in September 1942. At the end of July, Roosevelt sent a delegation to London, headed by Harry Hopkins, to persuade the British to cooperate. Their case was rejected outright. Churchill, backed by the British Chiefs of Staff, condemned the Cherbourg plan as too weak to have a hope of

On 14 May, 1943, the third anniversary of the formation of Britain's Home Guard, Churchill marked the event with a broadcast from the White House in Washington. Churchill (above) as he arrives at the Quebec Conference of August 1943.

holding off the inevitable German counterattack. Reluctantly, the Americans backed down.

Instead, it was decided that the Allies would mount an offensive on the Mediterranean coast of North Africa, which seemed the most promising area in which to challenge the Germans and their Italian allies. Decisive action in North Africa was not long in coming. In October 1942, the British Eighth Army triumphed at El Alamein in northern Egypt, forcing Erwin Rommel's Afrika Korps into a rapid retreat westwards. On 8 November, Operation Torch was launched and 60,500 Allied troops landed on the coasts of the French territories of Morocco and Algeria. Swiftly overcoming reistance from the Vichy French forces, they ensured that the first Anglo-American joint venture of the war proved a success.

Churchill now tried to revive plans for a cross-Channel invasion in 1943. But the Chiefs

Roosevelt and Churchill during the Casablanca Conference in January 1943. 'Meeting Franklin Roosevelt,' Churchill said, 'was like opening your first bottle of champagne; knowing him was like drinking it.'

of Staff informed the Prime Minister that this was impossible: although American troops had been arriving in Britain since the start of 1942, there were not yet enough to fulfil such a timetable. The Chiefs also argued that the Germans could rapidly reinforce the Atlantic Wall, the line of defences along the northern coast of France, by using the excellent rail system of continental Europe: German troops could be rapidly relocated so that they were prepared for any Allied invasion.

The potential for disaster had already been revealed at Dieppe, where a mainly Canadian force of 6000 men landed on 19 August, 1942. Designated a 'reconnaissance in force', the raid was designed as a trial run to establish a beach-head and capture a French port. What it showed was that a successful assault would require a more sophisticated and technologically advanced operation than the Canadians had to offer. Battered by German counter-attacks, without proper communications or air cover of their own, nearly two-thirds of the Canadians were killed, injured or captured.

With this costly lesson in mind, the Chiefs of Staff thought it far better to invade Europe from the south, with a landing in Italy, using the troops already fighting in North Africa. Once Italy was forced out of the war, the Balkans could be the next target. Their opinion was endorsed when Churchill, Roosevelt and their respective Chiefs of Staff met in Casablanca, on the Atlantic coast of French Morocco, on 14 January, 1943. At the conference, neither the Italian nor the cross-Channel venture was sanctioned for action that year, even though the latter was also favoured by General Marshall and other American service chiefs. Instead, it was decided that once final victory had been achieved in North Africa, an assault would be launched on Sicily as a precursor to an invasion of the Italian mainland. But the

En route to the White House in Washington on 4 June, 1943, Roosevelt and Churchill celebrate the news they have just received that the fighting between Allied and Axis forces in North Africa has come to an end.

CHURCHILL BROADCASTS TO THE WORLD, 29 NOVEMBER, 1942

Two Sundays ago, all the bells rang to celebrate the victory of our desert Army at Alamein. Here was a martial episode in British history which deserved a special recognition. But the bells also carried with their clashing joyous peals our thanksgiving that, in spite of all our errors and shortcomings, we have been brought nearer to the frontiers of deliverance ....

At the Quebec Conference, in September 1943, Canadian Prime Minister Mackenzie King (seated left), President Roosevelt (seated middle) and Winston Churchill discussed the appointment of a commander for the invasion of Europe. Churchill wantd Brooke to be in charge but Roosevelt insisted that the position go to an American.

ILLNESS AND CONVALESCENCE

It was an idyllic interlude at a taxing time. The Casablanca Conference and the two weeks Churchill spent touring British army units in the Middle East before flying home to Britain proved exhausting. He arrived back in London on 7 February feeling unwell, and nine days later developed a bout of pneumonia. Churchill refused to stop working and defied a temperature of 102 degrees to dictate a seven-page letter to the king explaining Anglo-American co-operation in Tunisia.

Getting well fast became Churchill's chief objective. 'I was very struck by his immense vigour and enthusiasm, his determination to get over his illness as quickly as possible,' his nurse Doris Miles later remembered. 'He told me that he ate and drank too much – roast beef for breakfast – and took no exercise, but was fitter than "old so-and-so who is two years younger than me". He loved watching films, particularly newsreels, and was delighted if he featured in them.'

FURY AT DELAYS

In April and May 1943 the news of developments in North Africa made Churchill more eager than ever to shake off his illness. The Germans and Italians had been fighting hard to defend their positions along the Tunisian coastline, but

leaders did agree that the cross-Channel attack would take place in early 1944, and Roosevelt promised that 938,000 American troops would be stationed in Britain by the end of 1943, in preparation for it.

At Casablanca, Churchill, Roosevelt and their advisers also decided the nature of the victory which the British and Americans meant to impose on their enemies: not an armistice or a negotiated peace, but unconditional surrender, first for the Italians and the Germans, and then the Japanese.

After the talks ended on 23 January, Churchill and Roosevelt took a brief break from the talk of war. Together, they drove inland to Marrakech, where they watched the sun flushing the sky with orange as it set beyond the peaks of the Atlas Mountains. 'The most lovely spot in the world,' was how Churchill described it. Entranced by the beauty around him, Churchill stayed on in Marrakech and spent an afternoon painting a view of the mountains. It was his only painting of the war years.

His nurse remembered: 'He told me that he ate and drank too much – roast beef for breakfast – and took no exercise, but was fitter than "old so-and-so who is two years younger than me"'.

During the Quebec Conference of 1943, Churchill toured the city and was mobbed by cheering crowds wherever he went. For Canadians, Churchill was a great hero who fought hard to preserve the democratic freedoms they valued. Today, admiration for Churchill remains strong throughout the world.

On 30 January, 1943, Churchill flew from Cairo to Turkey, where he met President Ismet Inönü near Adana. Churchill was convinced that he could persuade Inönü to bring Turkey into the war against Germany. But despite his concerted efforts, Turkey remained neutral throughout the war.

gradually they were being prised away and on 12 May their resistance came to an end. More than 240,000 Germans and Italians were taken prisoner. Churchill, who was on board the liner *Queen Mary* on his way to another meeting with Roosevelt, was elated when the news was signalled to him. He gave orders once again for church bells throughout Britain to be rung in celebration.

Now that North Africa was in Allied hands the way was clear to proceed with the invasion of Sicily, as agreed at Casablanca. But to Churchill's dismay the American General Dwight D Eisenhower, who had been in overall command of the Allied forces in North Africa, announced that he wanted to delay the Sicilian campaign for three or four months. Eisenhower's reason was the unexpected arrival of two German divisions on Sicily, in addition to the six Italian divisions already known to be on the

island. The British Joint Planning Committee shared his caution, but Churchill was furious and made no secret of his anger.

'I trust the Chiefs of Staff will not accept these pusillanimous and defeatist doctrines from whomever they come,' he raged. 'Such an attitude would make us the laughing stock of the world ....' What would happen, Churchill asked sarcastically, if two German divisions met Eisenhower 'at any of the other places he may propose .... What Stalin would think of this when he has 185 German divisions on his front, I cannot imagine.'

Churchill was not alone in his fury. The British and American Joint Chiefs were equally incensed and gave orders that the invasion of Sicily should go forward as planned. The *Queen Mary*, with Churchill aboard, reached New York on 11 May and the Joint Chiefs' decision was endorsed in Washington during his talks with Roosevelt. Sacrifices now had to be made. The next Arctic convoys to Murmansk were cancelled: the ships intended to sail with them as escorts were required for Sicily. The campaign also delayed the cross-Channel landing by requisitioning the transports earmarked for France, but compensation came in November 1943, when the date of May 1944 was finally fixed for the invasion of northern France.

SUCCESS IN SICILY

The Allied attack on Sicily, codenamed Operation Husky, began on 10 July, 1943, five weeks after Churchill returned home. He sat up until the small hours playing cards with his daughter-in-law Pamela, Randolph's wife, who afterwards recalled a 'very, very tense and torturous' night. 'We settled down to play bezique, which he loved,' Pamela remembered, 'and then one of the Private Secretaries came in to say that the winds had got up and they had delayed the landings, they did not know for how long. So we played bezique through the night and every now and again, he would put down the cards and he would say, "So many brave young men going to their death tonight. It is a grave responsibility." … we would go on playing bezique but he would always set down the cards and talk about the young people and sacrifices that they were being asked to make.' News that the landings had taken place came through at last at four in the morning.

The campaign in Sicily was a brief one, lasting only 38 days, but its success was overwhelming. Benito Mussolini, the dictator of Italy for 21 years, was forced to resign on 25 July and hand over the government to Field Marshal Pietro Badoglio. Eisenhower's fears about the two German divisions on Sicily proved excessive. By

CHURCHILL ADDRESSES THE BRITISH 'DESERT ARMY' IN TRIPOLI, LIBYA, 3 FEBRUARY, 1943

Let me assure you, soldiers and airmen, that your fellow countrymen regard your … work with admiration and gratitude and that after the War when a man is asked what he did, it will be quite sufficient for him to say 'I marched and fought with the Desert Army'. And when history is written and all the facts are known, your feats will gleam and glow and will be a source of song and story long after we who are gathered here have passed away.

On 30 June, 1943, Churchill received the Freedom of the City of London, an award bestowed on those who have served in an exceptional capacity. In celebration, Churchill rode through the City with his family.

In a rousing speech to a Joint Session of Congress in the United States on 19 May, 1943, Churchill urged his American allies to remain steadfast and strong in their duty to mankind.

17 August, when American and British forces were approaching Messina at the eastern tip of the island, the German and Italian forces were evacuated across the Strait of Messina to Reggio Calabria in the 'toe' of mainland Italy. Over 40,000 German and 60,000 Italian troops managed to get away, with 47 tanks, 10,000 vehicles and many thousands of tons of supplies. As Churchill had feared, the Allied victory was expensive, costing 20,000 casualties. Around 12,000 Germans and 147,000 Italians were killed or captured.

BOUND FOR QUEBEC

Once Allied success in Sicily seemed guaranteed, Churchill turned his attention to another problem: the increasingly strained relations between Britain and the United States. After returning from his third journey to America, Churchill told the House of Commons: 'All sorts of divergences, all sorts of differences of outlook and all sorts of awkward little jars necessarily occur as we roll ponderously forward together along the rough and broken road of war.' Characteristically, Churchill continued on a more positive note: 'But none of these makes the slightest difference to our ever-growing concert and unity. There are none of them that cannot be settled face to face by heart-to-heart talks and patient argument.'

The Americans had proposed that the Mediterranean island of Sardinia, rather than Italy, should be the next target after Sicily, but Churchill disagreed. Oliver Harvey, a Foreign Office diplomat, believed that at the back of Churchill's mind was the fear that the Americans might abandon the campaign in Europe. 'He is anxious to pin the Americans down,' Harvey wrote in his diary, 'before they pull out their

landing craft and send off their ships to the Pacific.' Churchill decided that a fourth meeting with President Roosevelt was needed and, accompanied by Clementine, he boarded the *Queen Mary* on 5 August, bound for Quebec in Canada. While he was there, he thought to keep Josef Stalin happy by sending him a 'small stereoscopic machine': this enabled the Soviet leader to view highly realistic 3D slides showing bombed-out German cities as they appeared after British air raids.

The Quebec Conference lasted only two days, but a firm plan for the future was worked out. It was confirmed that an amphibious invasion of northern France would take place in May 1944, as a prelude to an assault on Nazi Germany itself. The Allies also agreed on a diversionary assault on the Riviera coast of southern France

CHURCHILL ADDRESSES THE US CONGRESS, 19 MAY, 1943

We have surmounted many serious dangers, but there is one grave danger which will go along with us till the end; that danger is the undue prolongation of the War. No one can tell what new complications and perils might arise in four or five more years of war. And it is in the dragging out of the War at enormous expense, until the democracies are tired or bored or split, that the main hopes of Germany and Japan must now reside. We must destroy this hope, as we have destroyed so many others, and for that purpose, we must beware of every topic, however attractive, and every tendency, however natural, which turns our minds and energies from this supreme objective of ... victory .... By singleness of purpose, by steadfastness of conduct, by tenacity and endurance such as we have so far displayed – by these and only by these can we discharge our duty to the future of the world and the destiny of Man.

Stalin had every reason to look pleased with himself at the Tehran Conference of 1943, where he had succeeded in outmanoeuvring Churchill over his plan for an invasion of Europe through Yugoslavia.

to force the Germans to move troops and weaponry away from the Channel. The campaign in Italy was to be downgraded in importance: the capture of Rome was the principal target, but the Allied advance up the length of Italy was to reach no further than Pisa in Tuscany, some 286 miles north of the capital. In the Pacific and south-east Asia, the Allies agreed that Japan would be defeated within a year of Germany's downfall.

A BRIEF RESPITE

By the time the negotiations were completed, on 24 August, Churchill was exhausted. He left Quebec to spend a few quiet days at a fishing camp in the Laurentian mountains. It was peaceful, and an ideal place to get a view of the *Aurora Borealis*, the spectacular Northern Lights. Churchill came out onto a riverside pier to gaze up at the curtains of sparkling light that painted the night sky high above. His doctor, who was with him, remarked: 'This quiet life is doing him good, but he feels he is playing truant.'

When Churchill returned to Britain the following month he found a catalogue of events unfolding. Italy had surrendered on 3 September and was invaded by Allied forces the same day, although German forces continued to fight on in Italy for some time afterwards. Four weeks later, the Allies entered Naples. The Mediterranean islands of Corsica and Sardinia were captured after only a token fight.

In the Battle of the Atlantic, German U-boats were using a new acoustic torpedo that found its target by picking up sounds from engines or propellers. But it came too late to reverse the balance of power in the Atlantic, which was by now firmly on the side of the Anglo-Americans. And in Russia, a huge tank battle at Kursk in July ended in defeat for the Nazis, setting the Red Army on an advance that would not halt until they reached Berlin.

Churchill came up with a plan to clear the path to Allied victory with an assault on the island of Rhodes in the Aegean Sea. Rhodes had

been ruled by the Italians since 1912 and, as long as it remained unconquered, could be used by the Germans as a base to endanger the Allies' campaign in the Italian peninsula. Churchill became enormously excited over his scheme and seemed to lose sight of other priorities.

A FIXATION WITH RHODES

Alan Brooke was furious with him and confided to his diary: 'I can control him no more. He has worked himself into a frenzy of excitement about

The Red Army's victory in the Battle of Stalingrad in January 1943 swung the balance of the war in the Soviets' favour. At the Tehran Conference, Churchill marked the Soviet success by presenting Stalin with a sword of honour.

the Rhodes attack, has magnified its importance so that he can no longer see anything else and has set himself on capturing this one island even at the expense of endangering his relations with the President and the Americans and the future of the Italian campaign. He refused to listen to any arguments or to see any dangers.'

Brooke would not endorse the Rhodes venture and President Roosevelt also opposed it. Churchill became so upset that he even spoke darkly about 'chucking it in'. He told his secretary Marian Holmes, 'The difficulty is not in winning the War, it is in persuading people to let you win it.'

Roosevelt would not budge and became irritated that Churchill should seek to renege on agreements already concluded at Quebec. He sent Churchill a telegram insisting that there must be no diversion of forces or equipment that could compromise the Allied advance in Italy or the cross-Channel assault, now codenamed Operation Overlord.

ODD MAN OUT

Stalin had his own vested interest in Overlord, the 'second front' he sorely needed to distract the Germans from the war in Russia. In November

Churchill spent his 69th birthday in Tehran. That evening, he hosted a dinner for the delegates and numerous toasts were drunk. 'I drink to the Proletarian masses,' Churchill said, for Stalin's benefit.

CHURCHILL ON AMERICAN ISOLATIONISM 6 SEPTEMBER, 1943

Twice in my lifetime, the long arm of destiny has searched across the oceans and involved the entire life and manhood of the United States in a deadly struggle. There was no use in saying 'We don't want it; we won't have it; our forebears left Europe to avoid these quarrels; we have founded a new world which has no contact with the old.' There was no use in that. The long arm reaches out remorselessly, and everyone's existence, environment and outlook undergo a swift and irresistible change .... The price of greatness is responsibility. If the people of the United States had continued ... absorbed in their own affairs and a factor of no consequence in the movement of the world, they might have remained forgotten and undisturbed beyond their protecting oceans. But one cannot rise to be in many ways the leading community in the civilised world without being involved in its problems, without being convulsed by its agonies and inspired by its causes.

1943 the commitment to the second front was confirmed at the Tehran Conference in Persia, where Churchill, Roosevelt and Stalin – the 'Big Three' as they were called by the newspapers – met together for the first time. The principle of a 'second front' was one thing, but its location was quite another. Churchill's idea of a 'second front' was an invasion through Yugoslavia. Stalin interpreted this as a British attempt to secure Vienna and Belgrade, the Austrian and Yugoslav capitals, before the Soviet Red Army was able to reach them.

Stalin categorically opposed Churchill's plan, and Roosevelt agreed with him. Encouraged by his own service chiefs, Roosevelt favoured an Allied invasion of northwest France. Although he would have preferred a direct strike against Germany from the west, this satisfied Stalin who also agreed to an invasion date in May 1944. Churchill was outmanoeuvred and outvoted. There was something predictable about this outcome. Before the conference began, Stalin had virtually hijacked the American President: he insisted that he stay at the Soviet rather than the British legation in Tehran, ostensibly to preserve him from a possible assassination attempt. By this means, contact between Churchill and Roosevelt was effectively reduced. Later on during the conference, Stalin and Roosevelt contrived to confer together in Churchill's absence. In addition, Roosevelt turned down Churchill's invitation to luncheon in case Stalin thought they were ganging up on him. That

same afternoon, Roosevelt and Stalin had another meeting, again without Churchill.

Despite this, the three managed to agree on the fate of Germany in anticipation of an ultimate Allied victory. The defeated Germany would be divided into five small autonomous states. Churchill was particularly keen that Prussia, long the core of German militarism, should be isolated.

Churchill left Tehran for Cairo on 2 December. He had been suffering from exhaustion again but insisted on holding daily meetings with his advisers to discuss supplying aid to the anti-Nazi partisans in Yugoslavia, Greece and Albania. On 10 December he flew to Carthage in Tunisia, more than eight hours from Cairo by air, where he became very unwell.

ILL HEALTH

'They took him out of the plane,' Brooke remembered, 'and he sat on his suitcase in a very cold morning wind, looking like nothing on earth.' Churchill had caught pneumonia once again, and, worse still, on 15 December he suffered a second heart attack. Like the first, it was mild, but was followed by another two days later. 'Papa is very upset,' Clementine wrote to Mary after flying to Carthage to be with her husband, 'as he is beginning to see that he cannot get well in a few days and that he will have to lead what for him is a dreary monotonous life with no emotions or excitements.'

The mood soon passed. Churchill held several bedside conferences, with visits from General

Roosevelt and Churchill met the Chinese Commander-in-Chief General Chiang Kai-shek and his wife in Cairo in November 1943. China had been at war since 7 July, 1937, when it was invaded by Japan. China's contribution to the Allied war effort was hamstrung by the fact that Chiang's Nationalist government, which had already been weakened by corruption and inflation, was under threat from rival Communists.

Eisenhower and his deputy, the British General Sir Harold Alexander. The three of them discussed the forthcoming amphibious landing at Anzio, 33 miles south of Rome, which was intended to prepare the way for the capture of the Italian capital. By Christmas, Churchill was openly ignoring medical advice. 'The doctors are quite unable to control him,' wrote John Martin, Churchill's Principal Private Secretary, 'and the cigars have now returned.'

Harold Macmillan, Minister of State for North Africa and a future Prime Minister, came to visit Churchill and afterwards wrote in his diary: 'He took my hand in his in a most fatherly way and said: "Come and see me again before I leave Africa … " He really is a remarkable man. Although he can be so tiresome and pigheaded, there is no one like him.'

FULL VIGOUR RETURNED

Churchill convalesced at Marrakech after defying his doctors by flying there at what they considered an unsafe altitude. His aircraft had to climb above 3000 m (9846 ft) to pass over the mountains, requiring him to wear his oxygen mask again. On the last day of the year General Eisenhower and General Bernard Montgomery, the victor of El Alamein in 1942, arrived in Marrakech to discuss Operation Overlord with Churchill. Clementine was with him, and on New Year's Day 1944, he went to her room with good news. 'I am so happy,' he told her, 'I feel so much better.' To prove it, Churchill took a two-hour drive with Montgomery to the Atlas mountains, where they ate a picnic lunch and admired the view.

On 18 January, 1944 Churchill was back in London. The same day, he was in the House of Commons for the regular question and answer session known as Prime Minister's Questions, then met his War Cabinet and lunched with the king at Buckingham Palace. In his 70th year and despite his heart problems, Churchill seemed to have returned to full vigour and a full timetable. But before the end of the month another crisis emerged.

Churchill and other war leaders test out the US Army's new rifle in 1943. General Dwight D Eisenhower (left) was a desk general who had never taken part in a battle. But Lieutenant General Omar Bradley (right) was a crack shot, having gained his expertise while hunting with his father as a small boy.

The amphibious invasion at Anzio, which took place on 22 January, had failed six days later when faced with fierce German resistance.

'We hoped to land a wild cat that would tear the bowels out of the Boche,' Churchill commented, ' instead we have stranded a vast whale with its tail flopping about in the water.' Four months passed before the Allied troops managed to break the German defences and fight their way out of the beach-head and onto the road that led to Rome.

As 1944 progressed, Operation Overlord increasingly dominated Churchill's workload. He was in regular discussions with General Eisenhower, who had been appointed Supreme

Allied Commander in Western Europe in 1943, and chaired the weekly Overlord Committee of the War Cabinet. General Hastings Ismay, Churchill's link with the Chiefs of Staff, described what it was like to sit in session at committee meetings with a Prime Minister turned taskmaster. 'His fiery energy and undisputed authority dominated the proceedings,' Ismay remembered. 'The seemingly slothful or obstructive were tongue-lashed; competing differences were reconciled; priorities were settled; difficulties which at first appeared insuperable were overcome and decisions were translated into immediate action.'

No detail of the complex arrangements for Overlord escaped Churchill's attention – the naval bombardment and glider-borne assault preceding the beach landings, the air support and the artificial harbours where supplies and reinforcements were to be unloaded. The strain of the last few months before the Normandy invasion proved extremely tiring for Churchill. The pressure mounted when intelligence sources and Bletchley Park decrypts revealed that the Germans were developing pioneering rocket technology, which they planned to use in an attack on Britain.

IMMINENT THREAT

In a broadcast made on 26 March, Churchill spoke in carefully veiled terms about the forthcoming invasion of France, but included a more direct warning of the imminent threat to Britain. 'The hour of our greatest effort and action is approaching. We march with valiant Allies who count on us as we count on them. The flashing eyes of all our soldiers, sailors and airmen must be fixed upon the enemy on their front. The only homeward road for all of us lies through the arch of victory .... And here I must warn you that ... we may also ourselves be the object of new forms of attack from the enemy. Britain can take it. She has never flinched or failed. And when the signal is given, the whole circle of avenging nations will hurl themselves upon the foe and batter out the life of the cruellest tyranny which has ever sought to bar the progress of mankind.'

Churchill met General Charles De Gaulle in Marrakech on 13 January, 1944. With difficulty, Churchill managed to persuade the arrogant and stubborn De Gaulle not to persecute former supporters of the collaborationist Vichy regime who had controlled Morocco.

Churchill's wording was, as always, majestic and rousing, but listeners discerned exhaustion in his delivery. 'People seem to think that Winston's broadcast ... was that of a worn and petulant old man,' author and publisher Harold Nicolson wrote in his diary.

General Brooke, who saw Churchill almost every day, became worried about him. 'I am afraid that he is losing ground rapidly,' he wrote. 'He seems incapable of concentrating for a few minutes on end, and keeps wandering continuously ... he was looking old and lacking a great deal of his usual vitality.' Even so, Brooke concluded: 'I have never yet heard him admit that he was beginning to fail.'

Churchill drove himself hard and his level of activity barely faltered. He held prolonged talks with British and American officers about their roles in the Normandy invasion. He worried about the French civilians who would be killed in the pre-invasion bombing of the railways in northern France. He fretted over the slow progress being made in Italy. He also became alarmed at signs that Stalin was intent on spreading communism into eastern Europe and protested when Soviet forces advancing into Romania in the spring of 1944 arrested anti-communists along with Fascist leaders. 'Never forget,' Churchill told Anthony Eden, 'that Bolsheviks are crocodiles.'

> 'The hour of our greatest effort and action is approaching. We march with valiant Allies who count on us as we count on them. The flashing eyes of all our soldiers, sailors and airmen must be fixed upon the enemy on their front. The only homeward road for all of us lies through the arch of victory ... '

WATCHING THE WEATHER

The start of Operation Overlord, which would become known as 'D-Day', had initially been fixed for May 1944 but was delayed. On the evening of 4 June Churchill arrived in London. He was greatly cheered by good news from Italy, where the Allied advance out of Anzio had begun at last. At 10:30PM that evening, he summoned his secretary Marian Holmes and sat working and dictating until 3:45AM the next morning. The date planned for D-Day, 5 June, had arrived. So had another, anxiously awaited, piece of news: during the night, Churchill was told that Rome had fallen. Ecstatic crowds, Churchill learned, were lining the streets of the Italian capital to cheer the British and Americans, and shower them with flowers as they drove past.

The weather in the English Channel, often changeable, turned to rainstorms and high winds on 5 June and General Eisenhower decided to postpone the Normandy invasion by one day. An important factor in his decision was the Germans' belief that the weather would not clear for the next four or five days. They were so confident of this that General Erwin Rommel, in command of the defences in northern France, returned to Germany on leave.

That night, Churchill and Clementine went to the Map Room at the Number 10 Annexe. Clementine told her husband: 'I feel so much for you at this agonising moment, so full of suspense.' Churchill studied the maps showing the dispositions of the German forces in Normandy, compiled from decoded Enigma messages, and the projected Allied dispositions. Churchill turned to Clementine. 'Do you realise,' he said, 'that by the time you wake up in the morning, 20,000 men may have been killed?'

THE PATH TO VICTORY

IN 1944, CHURCHILL WATCHED BATTLES IN FRANCE, ITALY AND
ON THE RHINE BORDER OF GERMANY. AT HOME, BRITAIN FACED
THE V-1 FLYING BOMB AND THE V-2 ROCKET, WHILE TO
CHURCHILL'S DISTRESS MUCH OF EUROPE FACED THE THREAT OF
COMMUNIST DOMINANCE. THE PROSPECT MARRED
HIS SATISFACTION AS WORLD WAR II DREW TO A
CLOSE IN THE SPRING OF 1945.

AFTER ONLY A FEW HOURS' SLEEP, Churchill was
back in the Map Room on the morning of 6 June,
watching the charts gradually transform as the action
from the Normandy beaches was plotted in front of
him. Initial news of the landings was encouraging and
at midday Churchill was able to make a confident
speech to the House of Commons.

'I have to announce to the House,' he told MPs, 'that
during the night and the early hours of this morning, the
first of the series of landings in force upon the European Continent
has taken place .... An immense armada of upwards of 4000 ships,
together with several thousand smaller craft, crossed the Channel ....
The fire of the shore batteries has been largely quelled .... So far, the
commanders who are engaged report that everything is proceeding
according to plan .... This vast operation is undoubtedly the most
complicated and difficult that has ever taken place.'

The success of the D-Day invasion of Normandy was greeted
with euphoria by the British public, to whom the downfall of Nazi
Germany now appeared imminent. They were mistaken. Another
long and costly year would pass until victory could be secured.

*In August 1944, Churchill (left) toured the battle areas in
Italy and France, staying in Florence, Italy, which the
German forces had evacuated on 10 August.
During his stay in Italy, Churchill inspected the 4th
Queen's Own Hussars (above). The regiment was
equipped with Sherman tanks modified to carry troops,
known as 'Kangaroos'.*

Six days after D-Day, Churchill crossed the Channel on board a destroyer to see the Normandy beach-heads for himself. It was only a day trip, but it was packed with action and Churchill relished the danger. At Courselles sur Mer, Churchill watched a Luftwaffe raid on the harbour, he saw landing craft unloading lorries, tanks and guns, and he witnessed Royal Navy ships bombarding German positions.

The destroyer was about to head back to England when Churchill suggested to Admiral Sir Philip Vian, who was accompanying him: 'Since we are so near, why shouldn't we have a plug at them ourselves?' The ship was within range of enemy artillery, but Vian complied. 'This is the only time I have ever been on board a naval vessel when she fired in anger,' Churchill commented later. 'I admired the Admiral's sporting spirit.'

LONDON UNDER ATTACK

That same evening, Churchill was back at the Annexe, dining with Clementine and Mary, when news came that the long-feared rocket attack on Britain was imminent. The Germans had 27 rocket-powered 'flying bombs', the *Vergeltungswaffe* 1 (V-1), ready to launch from France. Four reached London, coming in over the capital with an unforgettable low, throaty roar. Once the engine cut out, the V-1s lost momentum, crashed to earth and exploded. Two Londoners were killed in the first attack. The next night, when 50 V-1s reached London, Churchill and two of his private secretaries, Charles Dodd and John Peck, risked leaving the Annexe to witness the scene. Charles Dodd recalled that the episode 'exemplified the Prime Minister's energy and (hair-raising!) disregard for personal danger.' Churchill sent an insouciant message to Stalin, which read: 'We had a noisy night'.

The Allied landings on the beaches of Normandy on 6 June, 1944 were a huge operation, involving 5000 ships on the first day alone.

Defence was soon organised. Some V-1s were shot down by anti-aircraft batteries. Intrepid RAF pilots destroyed others by flying alongside, wingtip beneath wingtip, flinging the V-1s off-course as the pilots banked away. The combined effort disposed of 200 of the 700 V-1s launched on London in the first week of the attacks, but 526 civilians were killed. Churchill's response was defiant. The First Sea Lord, Admiral Sir Andrew Cunningham, wrote in his diary after an emergency staff conference that the Prime Minister 'said the matter had to be put robustly to the populace, that their tribulations were part of the battle in France and that they should be very glad to share in the soldiers' dangers.'

Churchill was mulling over ways of retaliating that would also halt flying bomb production and came up with some characteristically idiosyncratic ideas, such as the use of poisonous mustard gas. Churchill wrote in a note to the Chiefs of Staff: 'We could drench the cities of the Ruhr and many other cities in Germany in such a way that most of the population would be requiring constant medical attention. We could stop all work at the flying bomb starting points.' The Chiefs rejected the suggestion straight away. Gas, they told Churchill, was an inefficient weapon, difficult to control and unlikely to have the decisive effect he envisaged.

OPERATION ANVIL-DRAGOON

The V-1 campaign against Britain was relatively short-lived, petering out after only two months, by the end of August 1944. The Germans switched targets to the Belgian port of Antwerp, which was captured by British forces on 4 September. But Britain was not off the hook. On 8 September, the Germans launched another, much more powerful, weapon. The supersonic V-2 missile, a forerunner of post-war space rockets, fell out of the sky without sound or warning. The V-2 attacks on Britain lasted for 6 months, killing 2754, nearly 80 per cent of them in London.

Operation Anvil-Dragoon, the Allied invasion of southern France, took place at St Tropez on 15 August, 1944, but failed to distract the Germans from their defence of the Normandy coast as the Americans had hoped. There was no mass withdrawal of troops to head off the assault in the south and the German garrison stationed on the French Riviera quickly surrendered to the Allies. Within only four weeks, the Allied forces joined up with troops advancing from Normandy, where the breakout from the beach-heads had taken seven hard-fought weeks at the cost of more than 120,000 Allied casualties.

Churchill, who was on a tour of the battle areas in Normandy and Italy, watched the invasion of southern France from the deck of the destroyer *HMS Kimberley*. He saw 'the panorama of the beautiful shore with smoke rising from many fires started by the shelling and artificial smoke being loosed by the landing troops and the

CHURCHILL ON VICTORY IN THE BATTLE OF NORMANDY, 28 SEPTEMBER, 1944

Little more than seven weeks have passed since we rose for the summer vacation, but this short period has completely changed the face of the war in Europe. When we separated, the Anglo-American armies were still penned in the narrow bridgehead and strip of coast from the base of the Cherbourg peninsula to the approaches to Caen … the Germany Army in the West was still hopeful of preventing us from striking out into the fields of France and the battle of Normandy, which had been raging bloodily from the date of the landing, had not reached any decisive conclusion. What a transformation now meets our eyes! Not only Paris, but practically the whole of France, has been liberated …. Belgium has been rescued, part of Holland is already free and the foul enemy, who for four years inflicted his cruelties and oppression upon these countries, has fled ….

landing-craft drawn up upon the shore.' Churchill found the invasion 'rather dull', for instead of a day-long bombardment from sea and air, the Germans' onshore guns had been silenced by 8:00AM. Had he known the circumstances in advance, he wrote to Clementine, he would have taken a picket boat and watched 'very much nearer to the actual beach'.

A PIECE OF THE ACTION

Churchill was better satisfied in Italy ten days later, when he stood with General Alexander on a high point above the German defence line around Florence as Allied forces attacked. 'Here one certainly could see all that was possible,' Churchill remembered. 'The Germans were firing with rifles and machine guns from thick scrub on the farther side of the valley, about 500 yards away. Our front line was beneath us. The firing was desultory and intermittent. But this was the nearest I got to the enemy and the time I heard the most bullets in the Second World War.'

On 12 June, 1944, six days after D-Day, Churchill crossed the Channel to witness the action for himself. He had wanted to go to Normandy with the invasion fleet, but was talked out of it by King George VI.

Churchill returned to Britain three days later on 29 August, but the month-long tour had been tiring and he succumbed to another bout of pneumonia. He was still recovering in bed on 3 September, when grave news reached him from Warsaw in Poland, where Polish insurgents were fighting a desperate battle against the Germans. Soviet forces were little more than 50 miles away, but had been ordered by Stalin not to interfere. The insurgents were attempting to establish a democratic government in Poland. Stalin meant the country to have a communist future and realised that the Germans would do his work for him by eliminating his potential opponents.

Churchill was enraged at Stalin's attitude and, despite a high fever, he called a Cabinet meeting

On 22 July, 1944, nine days after Caen was captured, Churchill visited the Normandy town with General Montgomery (second right) and the Canadian Lieutenant-General Guy Simonds (left). Caen had been a vital lynchpin in the German defences. The only town among the myriad villages in this part of France, Caen dominated the undulating plains on which it stood and was a vital railway centre and the hub of twelve major roads.

Churchill, accompanied by General Bernard Montgomery, speaks to British troops at Caen. It had been originally planned that Caen would be captured on D-Day itself, but the Allied advance was hampered by strong German resistance and difficult terrain. Caen was largely destroyed in the savage fighting that followed.

in the underground War Rooms. The Cabinet agreed that the situation in Warsaw was a scandal, but toned down their protest for the sake of preserving the alliance with the Soviet Union. In a carefully worded telegram, ministers told Stalin that his actions seemed 'at variance with the spirit of Allied co-operation to which you and we attach so much importance, both for the present and for the future.' The mild message had no effect and the insurgents in Warsaw were slaughtered while their city was laid waste all around them. It was a sombre lesson for the post-war future which Churchill would not forget.

Churchill's convalescence was still not complete when he embarked on the liner *Queen Mary* at Greenock, on the River Clyde, on 5 September, for another meeting with Roosevelt in Quebec. The liner had waited a week for Churchill to arrive and he was concerned to learn that, because of the delay, American GIs on board would lose seven days of home leave. Immediately, he sent Roosevelt a message requesting that the time be made up to them. 'It would be a pleasure to me if this could be announced before the end of the voyage and their anxiety relieved,' Churchill stated. Roosevelt complied at once.

THE ATOMIC BOMB

Churchill reached Quebec on 12 September. The same day, news arrived that American forces had crossed the frontier into Germany close to Aachen. This first breach into Nazi territory was a joyful moment, heralding the end of the regime.

The Americans had come to Quebec with a scenario for a post-war Germany already worked out. Roosevelt's Secretary of the Treasury, Henry Morganthau, proposed to shut down all of Germany's factories, break up its shipyards and return the country to a pre-industrial, agricultural state. It was a step designed to take Germany back at least two centuries and so ensure that the nation could never again challenge the rest of Europe.

In the summer of 1944, with the Red Army 15 miles from the city, the Warsaw uprising was crushed by the occupying German forces. Churchill, aware of the need to keep Stalin as an ally, tried to excuse the Russians' failure to help the Poles, earning him the enmity of the Polish people both during and after the war.

CHURCHILL ON DEMOCRACY, 8 DECEMBER, 1944

Democracy, I say, is not based on violence or terrorism, but on reason, on fair play, on freedom, on respecting other people's rights as well as their ambitions. Democracy is no harlot to be picked up in the street by a man with a tommy gun. I trust the people, the mass of the people, in almost any country, but I like to make sure that it is the people, and not a gang of bandits ... who think that by violence they can overturn constituted authority, in some cases ancient Parliaments, governments and States. (Democracy has a price). We are paying for it with our treasure and our blood. We are not paying for it with our honour or by defeat.

Roosevelt agreed to the idea, as did Churchill, but it was rejected by the US State Department and the future of post-war Germany remained undecided. Japan's future was also under discussion. The Americans had been developing an atomic bomb following an agreement made between Britain and the United States in June 1942. Work was due to be completed by August 1945, and at the Quebec Conference the Americans raised the possibility of using it against the

Churchill in Normandy talking with Montgomery (left). Churchill was on good terms with Montgomery, but could be irritated by his caution. Montgomery was reluctant to send his forces into battle unless they were fully prepared and his delays frustrated the Americans.

Japanese. Churchill was not convinced that this would be necessary. He believed that prolonged bombing and 'an ever increasing weight of explosives on their centres of population' would eventually overcome Japanese resistance.

NEGOTIATING WITH STALIN

Churchill sailed home on the *Queen Mary*, arriving at Greenock on 26 September. Eleven days later, he departed for Moscow, where he presented Stalin with proposals that he hoped would curtail the spreading tide of communist influence in southern Europe and the Balkans. The inexorable advance of the Soviet Army had liberated Romania, Bulgaria and Yugoslavia, and was about to free Hungary. Communist minorities, bidding to take power, were already active in all these countries. In Greece, a

civil war was developing between the royalist government and communist guerrillas even before the Germans started their withdrawal, which was completed in November 1944.

Churchill's plan proposed 'percentages of interest' for Britain and Russia in five countries. The Russians received 90 per cent interest in Romania, the British ten per cent. The proportions were reversed in Greece. In Hungary, Bulgaria and Yugoslavia, the proportions were equal. In addition, as a concession, Churchill offered to persuade Turkey to allow Russia free access through the Dardanelles to the Mediterranean. In exchange, Churchill asked Stalin for his word not to promote communism in Greece or Italy.

Churchill handed the paper containing these proposals to Stalin, who put a large tick on it and handed it back. Realising the imperialist nature of the proposals in what Churchill called 'a naughty document', he lightheartedly suggested to Stalin that they dispose of it: 'Might it not be thought rather cynical if it seemed we had disposed of these issues, so fateful to millions of people, in such an offhand manner?' Churchill asked. 'Let us burn the paper.' Stalin disagreed: 'No,' he replied, 'You keep it.'

The discussion became less light-hearted when they moved on to the question of Poland, where the Germans had now crushed resistance in Warsaw. The Polish government in exile in London had told Churchill that they would accept nothing less than complete independence. Stalin had his own communist nominees ready to take over the government in post-war Poland. Neither side would yield. Churchill, who later described

himself to the House of Commons as travelling 'from court to court like a wandering minstrel, always with the same song to sing', had to admit that no compromise was possible.

The countries of eastern Europe were 'seething with communism,' Churchill told Anthony Eden, '... only our influence with Russia prevents their actively stimulating this movement, deadly as I conceive it to the freedom of Mankind.' In eastern Germany many people had no intention of waiting to see what the Russians would do with the 'freedom of Mankind'. Millions fled westwards to escape the Russians' revenge for atrocities the Nazi forces had perpetrated in Russia. Churchill's compassion was roused.

'I am free to confess to you that my heart is saddened by the tales of masses of German women and children flying along the roads everywhere in 40-mile long columns ... before the advancing armies,' Churchill wrote to Clementine. 'I am clearly convinced that they deserve it; but that does not remove it from one's gaze. The misery of the whole world appals me and I fear increasingly that new struggles may arise out of this which we are successfully ending.'

> 'I am free to confess to you that my heart is saddened by the tales of masses of German women and children flying along the roads everywhere in 40-mile long columns ... before the advancing armies. I am clearly convinced that they deserve it; but that does not remove it from one's gaze.'

A FRAIL ROOSEVELT

The new struggles he feared were already evident and Stalin's expansionist ambitions became a central concern for Churchill. On 29 January, 1945, he left London on the first leg of his journey to Yalta, on the south coast of the Crimea in Russia, for a conference with Stalin and Roosevelt to discuss the growing problem.

Churchill first headed for Malta to discuss tactics at Yalta with Anthony Eden and the Chiefs of Staff. Churchill wanted positive action to prevent the Russians advancing too far into Europe and placing communist governments in the territories they conquered. In this context, Austria was his first concern. 'It is essential,' Churchill told the Chiefs of Staff, 'that we occupy as much of Austria as possible, as it is undesirable that more of western Europe than necessary should be occupied by the Russians.'

It was soon evident that Churchill would have to do most, if not all, of the hard work at Yalta. President Roosevelt arrived in Malta on 2 February in no state for hard political bargaining. Churchill was shocked at his frail appearance. Normally so lively and charismatic, Roosevelt had become pale, grey and painfully thin. A year earlier, his doctors had diagnosed serious heart and circulatory problems and the deterioration in his health was all too evident. The President attended a few meetings in Malta, but for the most part sat silent and dull-eyed.

Churchill, Roosevelt and their respective staffs departed for Yalta on 3 February. The conference was held at the Livadia Palace, which had once been a residence of the last Tsar of Russia, Nicholas II. The timetable was not a taxing one. Discussions did not begin until four in the afternoon and lasted until about nine in the evening. That allowed Churchill to follow his favourite routine: he liked to rise late in the morning, then enjoy an early lunch with a short nap afterwards.

'At Yalta ... [Roosevelt's] captivating smile, his gay and charming manner had not deserted him, but his face had a transparency, an air of purification and often there was a faraway look in his eyes. When I took my leave of him ... I must confess that I had an indefinable sense of fear that his health and his strength were on the ebb.'

BROKEN PROMISES

Agreement was easily reached on several of the issues discussed at Yalta. The three leaders were in accord over the policy of unconditional surrender first announced by Churchill and Roosevelt at Casablanca in January 1943. Stalin concurred with the American request that he declare war on Japan once Germany was defeated. Stalin also agreed to Churchill's request for a Soviet attack on Danzig, where the Germans had built a revolutionary new type of submarine that had already sunk ships in British waters. There was assent too over the arrangements for the occupation of Germany after the war: Britain, the United States, the Soviet Union and France were to govern their own zones, with Berlin falling under joint control.

The long-term treatment of Germany was a more controversial matter. Despite prolonged discussion, there was no consensus over the dismembering of the country into five small states, or the level of reparations the Germans would have to pay, or the procedures for dealing with war criminals – by judicial process or by summary execution without trial. 'The only bond of the victors is their common hate,' Churchill told Anthony Eden, fearing that the desire for revenge might dominate post-war policy in Europe.

There was no hope of agreement on the subject of Poland either. By the time the Yalta Conference took place, the Soviet Army had gained control of Poland and a large part of

In August 1944, members of the War Cabinet went to Buckingham Palace for a private meeting with King George VI. Clement Attlee (second from left) and Anthony Eden (behind Churchill) were both to succeed him in the post of Prime Minister.

eastern Europe and Stalin could do as he pleased in these conquered territories. Although Stalin did promise Churchill that the Poles could have free and fair elections within a month, he did not keep his word. Every promise Stalin made at Yalta concerning Poland was afterwards broken.

A SOMBRE COMPARISON

Churchill returned home via Alexandria, where the *USS Quincy*, with President Roosevelt on board, was berthed on its way back to the United States. Roosevelt, exhausted by the strain of the Yalta Conference, seemed to be fading fast. 'I felt he had a slender contact with life,' Churchill afterwards recalled. 'At Yalta ... his captivating smile, his gay and charming manner had not deserted him, but his face had a transparency, an air of purification and often there was a faraway look in his eyes. When I took my leave of him in Alexandria harbour, I must confess that I had an

indefinable sense of fear that his health and his strength were on the ebb.' Churchill and Roosevelt never saw each other again.

Churchill was back in Britain on 19 February, after an absence of three weeks. Decisions made at the Yalta Conference regarding the fate of Poland had stirred up controversy. Many Members of Parliament found it impossible to believe Stalin's assurance of free elections. Churchill was guardedly hopeful when he wrote: 'Personally, in spite of my anti-Communist convictions, I have good hopes that Russia, or at any rate Stalin, desires to work in harmony with the Western

CHURCHILL ON THE HUMANITARIAN ASPECTS OF UNCONDITIONAL SURRENDER, 18 JANUARY, 1945

I am clear that nothing should induce us to abandon the principle of unconditional surrender ... but the President of the United States and I ... have repeatedly declared that the enforcement of unconditional surrender upon the enemy in no way relieves the victorious powers of their obligations to humanity or of their duties as civilised and Christian nations .... We may now say to our foes 'We demand unconditional surrender, but you well know how strict are the moral limits within which our action is confined. We are no extirpators of nations, butchers of peoples. We make no bargain with you. We accord you nothing as a right. Abandon your resistance unconditionally. We remain bound by our customs and our nature.

democracies. The alternative would be despair about the long term future of the world.'

It was a front. Behind it, Churchill was depressed by a sombre comparison. Here he was, trusting Stalin to keep his word, and yet in both 1938 and 1939, another Prime Minister, Neville Chamberlain, had trusted and been betrayed by another dictator, Adolf Hitler.

STAKING OUT TERRITORY

News of Stalin's betrayal reached Churchill in the next weeks. Reports told of political thuggery in Romania, where the Soviets were using intimidation, backed by military force, to impose a communist government. In Poland non-communists were excluded from government. Political opposition was banned. Some 2000 priests, intellectuals and teachers were sent to Soviet labour camps. In March 1945, Churchill sent a telegram to President Roosevelt urging him to exert 'dogged pressure and persistence' in the cause of preserving Polish freedom. There was no response. By this time, Roosevelt was past all exertions.

At the end of March, soon after he returned from an extensive tour of the battle front along the River Rhine, Churchill's attention was diverted by another problem. General Eisenhower had decided on a change of plan for the campaign in Germany: he wanted to abandon the drive for Berlin for the sake of a more southerly advance through Leipzig to Dresden, moving as far as, but not beyond, the River Elbe. Eisenhower was not convinced of the importance of Berlin, either as an industrial target or a military centre. His plan focused instead on overcoming the

At the Yalta Conference in February 1945, Stalin cunningly used the meeting to stake Soviet claims to territory in eastern Europe.

Despite his busy schedule, Churchill still found time to enjoy a cup of tea with British Army gunners at an artillery observation point in March 1945, as airborne troops crossed the River Rhine and entered Germany.

resistance the Germans were putting up in the industrial cities of the south.

Churchill and the British chiefs of staff were thoroughly alarmed when they received the news. To them, Eisenhower's plan was a terrible strategic error. Not only would it allow the Russians to seize Berlin, but halting American troops at the River Elbe would give the Russians access to even more territory in the east and could even threaten the Austrian capital, Vienna.

THE DEATH OF A PRESIDENT

Churchill used all possible persuasions to make Eisenhower change his mind. 'I deem it highly important,' he cabled the American general, 'that we should shake hands with the Russians as far

east as possible.' Eisenhower was unmoved. His new plan went forward and on 11 April, his forces reached the River Elbe. Berlin was less than 70 miles away, but the American troops made no sign of advancing towards it. Churchill interpreted the situation in the grimmest terms. 'It is by no means certain,' he said, 'that we could count on Russia as a beneficent influence in Europe or as a willing partner in maintaining the peace of the world. Yet, at the end of the War, Russia will be left in a position of preponderant power and influence throughout the whole of Europe.'

On 12 April President Roosevelt died, shortly after suffering a stroke while on holiday at Warm Springs, Georgia. Churchill was deeply upset. His telegram to his friend Harry Hopkins read: 'I feel a very painful personal loss, quite apart from the ties of public action which bound us closely together. I had a true affection for Franklin.'

Churchill paid tribute to the President on the day of his funeral, 17 April. 'My friendship with the great man to whose work and fame we pay

On 25 March, 1945, Churchill visited the bridge over the River Rhine at Wesel, which had been bombed by allied forces. German artillery shells were falling close by and Churchill was within range of snipers. According to General Brooke, who accompanied him, Churchill enjoyed the excitement and danger, and when asked to leave by the officer in command of the area, he did so very reluctantly.

our tribute today began and ripened during this war,' Churchill told the House of Commons. ' ... I conceived an admiration for him as a statesman, a man of affairs and a war leader. I felt the utmost confidence in his upright, inspiring character and outlook, and a personal regard – affection I must say – for him beyond my power to express today. .... President Roosevelt's physical affliction lay heavily upon him. It was a marvel that he bore up

Churchill was profoundly upset by the death of Roosevelt on 12 April, 1945. He attended a memorial service at St Paul's Cathedral in London on 17 April, accompanied by his daughter Sarah (behind him).

against it through all the many years of tumult and storm. Not one man in ten million, stricken and crippled as he was, would have attempted to plunge into a life of physical and mental exertion and of hard, ceaseless political controversy .... ' Churchill concluded, 'it remains only to say that in Franklin Roosevelt there died the greatest American friend we have ever known and the greatest champion of freedom who has ever brought help and comfort from the New World to the Old.'

HORRIBLE REVELATIONS

By this time, Nazi concentration camps were being uncovered by the advancing American and British armies. Rumours of atrocities against Jews, gypsies, Slavs, homosexuals and others the Nazis considered racially or otherwise 'inferior' had been circulating since the early stages of the war. But the brutalities committed at Auschwitz,

CHURCHILL ON VICTORY IN EUROPE, 8 MAY, 1945

We may allow ourselves a brief period of rejoicing; but let us not forget for a moment the toil and efforts that lie ahead. Japan, with all her treachery and greed, remains unsubdued. The injury she has inflicted on Great Britain, the United States and other countries and her detestable cruelties, call for justice and retribution. We must ... devote all our strength and resources to the completion of our task, both at home and abroad. Advance, Britannia! Long live the cause of freedom! God save the King!

Bergen-Belsen and Buchenwald were not fully revealed until the camps were liberated. The death camps in Poland were the first to be freed by the Russians at the start of 1945. In April, American troops discovered more camps as they advanced deeper into Germany from the west. The press coverage, showing pictures of corpses piled high in the camp compounds and skeletal survivors, hollow-eyed and barely alive, shocked cinema audiences and newspaper readers around the world. Churchill received a graphic description of the scene at Buchenwald in a telephone call from General Eisenhower. He wrote to Clementine, 'Here we are all shocked by the most horrible revelations of German cruelty in the concentration camps ….' On 19 April, he told the Commons: 'No words can express the horror which is felt by His Majesty's Government and their principal allies at the proofs of these frightful crimes now daily coming into view.'

The war was fast drawing to its close. On 20 April, the US Seventh Army captured Nuremberg. The Russians entered Berlin on 23 April. On 30 April, Hitler committed suicide in his underground bunker beneath the grounds of the Berlin Chancellery. The Russians, advancing through the shattered, rubble-strewn streets, were only a few yards away. A week later, all German forces surrendered unconditionally. Hitler's Third Reich, which he had declared would last a thousand years, had finally gone down in blood, flames and ruin.

In May 1945, Berlin was a mass of ruined buildings – windowless walls were often all that remained standing after more than four years of bombing.

CHURCHILL IN OPPOSITION

THE YEAR 1945 BROUGHT BOTH TRIUMPH AND DISAPPOINTMENT FOR CHURCHILL. THE WAR IN EUROPE ENDED IN MAY, BUT IN JULY THE CONSERVATIVES WERE HEAVILY DEFEATED IN A GENERAL ELECTION. NOW IN OPPOSITION, CHURCHILL WAS DOGGED BY RUMOURS OF HIS ILL HEALTH, AND BY HIS FEARS OF COMMUNIST DOMINANCE IN EUROPE.

UNDER THE TERMS OF THE GERMAN SURRENDER, fighting was to cease at midnight on 8 May, 1945. Jubilant crowds packed the streets of cities and towns all over Britain to celebrate the end of the war.

On the morning of 8 May, Churchill worked on the victory broadcast he was to deliver that day. He worked in bed – a longstanding habit – but got up after a while and went to the Map Room. He was carrying a bottle of champagne, a large Gruyère cheese and a note addressed to Captain Pim, head of the Map Room, and his staff. The note read: 'To Captain Pim and his officers with the Prime Minister's compliments on Victory Day in Europe.'

That afternoon Churchill made his victory broadcast from 10 Downing Street outlining the details of the German surrender. In the evening he appeared, with members of his Cabinet, on the balcony of the Ministry of Health building in Whitehall to address the London crowds in person. The roadway and pavements below were jam-packed with people waiting to hear him speak.

Churchill (left) addresses the Conservative Party Conference in election year 1945. They suffered a 146-seat shortfall as Labour won a landslide victory. On holiday at Hendaye, France (above), Churchill and Clementine enjoy a welcome break.

'This is your victory!' Churchill began, only to be interrupted by an answering roar from the crowd: 'No, it's yours!'. He continued: 'It is the victory of the cause of freedom in every land. In all our long history, we have never seen a greater day than this .... Everyone, man or woman, has done their best. Everyone has tried. Neither the long years, nor the dangers, nor the fierce attacks of the enemy, have in any way weakened the independent resolve of the British nation .... My dear friends, this is your hour. This is not the victory of a party or of any class. It's a victory of the great British nation as a whole ... '

When, at last, the crowds let him go, Churchill returned to his office, where telegrams from around the world were piled high on his desk. The celebrations continued unabated for the next few days, but Churchill's attention had

Churchill and members of his wartime Cabinet greet the crowds on Victory in Europe Day, 8 May, 1945. Many people across the world regarded Churchill as a great hero, but once the war was over, British voters felt that he was out of touch with domestic issues.

General Eisenhower (right) received the Freedom of the City of London in June 1945. Despite their apparent cordiality, Churchill and Eisenhower were not always in accord, both during the war and after Eisenhower became US President in 1952.

already turned to other pressing concerns. The Russians were tightening their hold over eastern and central Europe, and the Balkans. Equally alarming was the news that the Americans planned to withdraw half their troops from central Germany and send them to the Pacific where Japan remained undefeated. Churchill tried to impress on Roosevelt's successor, President Harry S Truman, his own fears for the future of Europe. American troops must remain at least until it became possible to reach an understanding with the Russians. Otherwise, Churchill predicted, the Russians could 'in a very short time ... advance, if they chose, to the waters of the North Sea and the Atlantic.'

'We have yet to make sure that the simple and honourable purposes for which we entered the war are not brushed aside or overlooked in the months following our success.'

REFORM

Truman agreed that Stalin must be confronted and arranged a conference at Potsdam near Berlin. In a broadcast on 13 May, Churchill warned his listeners of the difficulties ahead. 'All our toils and troubles,' he said, 'are not yet over .... We have yet to make sure that the simple and honourable purposes for which we entered the war are not brushed aside or overlooked in the months following our success, and that the words "freedom, democracy" and "liberation" are not distorted from their true meaning as we have understood them.'

The Potsdam conference was arranged for 17 July, but before that there was another challenge to be faced. Churchill had hoped that his wartime

Churchill visited the ruins of Berlin in July 1945 and sat in Hitler's chair outside the bunker where two months earlier the Nazi Führer had killed himself as the Russian army closed in.

coalition government could continue in office until Japan was defeated. But the Labour Party were putting pressure on him to call a General Election, for its members were convinced they stood a good chance of victory.

The publication of the Beveridge Report in 1942 had provided the Labour Party with a strong base for their election campaign. Prepared by a committee led by the economist Sir William Beveridge, the report had outlined a radical new approach to Britain's social security system and supplied the blueprint for a future welfare state. It would provide unemployment insurance, free medical care, child benefit and old age pensions – benefits never before available on this scale. These reforms echoed Churchill's own welfare policies nearly 20 years earlier, but his commitment to social reform had been largely forgotten. Churchill was also still dogged by his reputation as an oppressor of the working classes, earned as

CHURCHILL ON SOCIALISM, 5 JUNE, 1945

Look how even today (the Socialists) hunger for controls of every kind, as if these were delectable foods instead of wartime inflictions and monstrosities. There is to be one State to which all are to be obedient in every act of their lives. This State is to be the arch-employer, the arch-planner, the arch-administrator and ruler and the arch-caucus-boss. How is the ordinary citizen or subject of the King to stand up against this formidable machine which, once it is in power, will prescribe for every one … where they are to work, what they are to work at, where they may go and what they may say, what views they are to hold and within what limits they may express them?

a result of his role in the General Strike of 1926. In the summer of 1945, Clement Attlee and his Labour colleagues were better able to present themselves as creators of the future welfare state.

The coalition government had to step down and on 23 May, at Buckingham Palace, Churchill tendered his resignation to George VI. He left the Palace as leader of a new caretaker government which, at the king's request, would govern Britain until parliamentary elections were concluded. Three days later, Churchill was already on the campaign trail. He chose as his central theme the perils of socialism – the basic creed of his Labour opponents – which he equated with communism.

'GESTAPO' MISJUDGMENT

Churchill misjudged the mood of the people. There was a widespread feeling, especially among the young men and women who had served in the armed forces, that the state should now focus on solving social problems and they welcomed the socialist measures the Labour Party was promising. But Churchill doggedly pursued his theme throughout the campaign. The broadcast he made on 4 June did more damage to his case than his opponents could hope to inflict themselves. 'My friends,' he said, 'I must tell you that a Socialist policy is abhorrent to the British ideas of freedom …. There can be no doubt that Socialism is inseparably interwoven with totalitarianism and the abject worship of the

Churchill was present at the first meeting of the 'Big Three' conference in Potsdam, Berlin in July 1945, but when the conference resumed in August the newly elected Labour Prime Minister, Clement Attlee, took his place after Churchill's surprise defeat in the General Election.

Although his party lost the 1945 election, Churchill won a huge majority (above) in a new constituency, Woodford. He won there again in the next election in 1950, and remained MP for Woodford until he retired from Parliament in 1964.

Miami was one of 20 universities to offer Churchill an honorary degree. He was presented with the degree by Dr Bowman Ashe, President of the University, at the ceremony in the Burdine Stadium in Miami on 4 March, 1946.

State. It is not alone that property in all its forms, is struck at, but that liberty, in all its forms, is challenged by the fundamental conceptions of Socialism .... (The Socialists) would have to fall back on some kind of Gestapo .... '

The 'Gestapo' accusation was one of the greatest miscalculations of Churchill's political career. His comparison of the Labour Party – whose leaders, Clement Attlee, Herbert Morrison and Ernest Bevin, had worked alongside him throughout the war – with the brutal Nazi secret police provoked embarrassment and outrage across the political spectrum. In later speeches and broadcasts, Churchill toned down his attacks on

socialism, trying to reassure voters of his commitment to the Beveridge Plan, but the 'Gestapo' label stuck and damaged his chances in the election.

Paradoxically, his own personal popularity remained unaffected. Wherever he was out in public, people lost no opportunity to show the affection they had for him. John Martin, who worked in Churchill's private office, was in a car with Churchill on the way to Chequers when they got caught up in a traffic jam outside the White City, a sports stadium in west London. 'The crowds were coming away from the greyhound races,' Martin wrote to his wife on 17 June. 'Immediately

he was surrounded by an extremely enthusiastic (crowd) ... not a sign of unfriendliness or opposition. It was a remarkable demonstration ....'

END OF THE ALLIANCE
The General Election took place on 5 July, 1945, but the results were delayed for three weeks, until the votes of service personnel overseas had been counted. The interval allowed Churchill to attend the Potsdam Conference, and to take a short holiday in France with his daughter Mary. The rigours of electioneering had left him feeling sad and tired. Fortunately, he had brought his easel, canvas and paints. 'The magic of painting soon laid hold of him,' Mary remembered, 'absorbing him for hours on end and banishing disturbing thoughts of either the present or the future.'

A week later Churchill and his daughter left for Potsdam, outside Berlin, for the conference which

opened on 17 July. At first, negotiations were straightforward. The 'Big Three' – Churchill, Stalin and, for the first time, President Truman – agreed the practical details for governing conquered Germany and approved, in principle, the reparations that were due to Russia and other countries which had suffered from Nazi aggression. They also created an International Military Tribunal to prosecute Nazi war criminals. But the conference did not fulfil Churchill's major objective: to curb the spread of communism.

Potsdam had come far too late. Russian dominance was already well established in central and eastern Europe and Stalin had no intention of allowing democratic elections, despite his promises at Yalta. The wartime alliance between East and West had come to an end.

President Truman (left) introduced Churchill to his audience at Fulton, Missouri where the former Prime Minister made his controversial 'Iron Curtain' speech on 5 March, 1946. Churchill was accused of being alarmist about the threat of communism in Europe.

ELECTION DEFEAT

So had Churchill's time as Prime Minister. He flew home on 25 July to learn the outcome of the election. The Conservatives had been decisively defeated, voted out by a 'landslide' Labour majority of 146 seats. The vote of the servicemen overseas, in which the lower ranks overwhelmingly voted Labour, had been the decisive factor.

Churchill was devastated by the result. Clementine attempted to console him, suggesting 'It may well be a blessing in disguise.' To which he replied, 'At the moment, it seems quite effectively disguised.' Anthony Eden's diary recorded Churchill's bitter disappointment: 'He was pretty wretched, poor old boy. Said he didn't feel any

In March 1946, Churchill (right) and Clementine (left) joined President Roosevelt's widow Eleanor (centre) to pay their respects at the flower-covered grave of the president at the Roosevelt family home at Hyde Park, New York.

more reconciled this morning, on the contrary it hurt more, like a wound which becomes more painful after the first shock.' Churchill had never been suited to the role of bystander, and the greatest pain of defeat was no longer being able to influence events. As he told his secretary Elizabeth Layton: 'I wanted to do the peace, too.'

In Potsdam the delegates had been certain that Churchill would return to resume negotiations after the election. They were astounded when Clement Attlee, the new Prime Minister, appeared instead.

On President Truman's orders, the war against Japan was brought to an abrupt and devastating conclusion when atomic bombs were dropped on Hiroshima on 6 August and on Nagasaki three days later. Japan surrendered unconditionally on

CHURCHILL'S STATEMENT FROM 10 DOWNING STREET AFTER HIS DEFEAT IN THE 1945 GENERAL ELECTION, 26 JULY, 1945

The decision of the British people has been recorded in the votes counted today. I have therefore laid down the charge which was placed upon me in darker times. I regret that I have not been permitted to finish the work against Japan. For this, however, all plans and preparations have been made, and the results may come much quicker than we have hitherto been entitled to expect. Immense responsibilities abroad and at home fall upon the new Government, and we must all hope that they will be successful in bearing them.

It only remains for me to express to the British people … my profound gratitude for the unflinching, unswerving support which they have given me during my task and for the many expressions of kindness which they have shown towards their servant.

15 August. Churchill believed that Japan had been the wrong target. The bombs, he said, should have been used to threaten the Russians and make them 'behave reasonably and decently in Europe'. Truman, Churchill concluded, showed 'weakness in (adopting) this policy'.

REWARDED WITH HONOURS

Time helped to soften Churchill's disappointment. Nine weeks after his defeat he went on a painting holiday in Italy, where he found a multitude of subjects to put on canvas. In a single week, he painted three scenes around Lake Como and began a fourth. When he was not painting, he was swimming or tasting the thrill of driving a speedboat across the lake.

The pleasant time Churchill spent in Italy soothed his bruised ego. 'I am much better in myself and am not worrying about anything,' he wrote to Clementine who was in London. 'This is the first time for very many years that I have been

completely out of the world …. I feel a great sense of relief which grows steadily, others having to face the hideous problems of the aftermath.' Perhaps, Churchill mused, Clementine had been right. 'It may all indeed be a "blessing in disguise",' he concluded.

Churchill's great achievements as a wartime leader had not been forgotten. He was heaped with honours – the Order of Merit from George VI, the Médaille Militaire from the French government, honorary US citizenship, and honorary degrees from several universities. Vast crowds gathered to cheer and laud him wherever he went. When he delivered a speech analysing the causes of World War II to the Belgian Senate in November 1946, exuberant crowds mobbed his car on the way to the Parliament building. The British Ambassador to Brussels, who was with him, afterwards recalled: 'I have never seen such excitement or enthusiasm. People broke through the police cordon, dodged the motorcycle escort which surrounded the car and threw their bouquets into the car if they were not actually successful in handing them to Mr Churchill. One girl leapt onto the running board, threw her arms round his neck and kissed him fervently.'

CONTROVERSIAL VIEWS

Churchill and Clementine had another warm reception when they arrived in New York on board the liner *Queen Elizabeth* on 14 January, 1946. Churchill was soon receiving 300 letters a day, which required the services of three full-time secretaries. Churchill and Clementine spent time relaxing at Miami Beach, and visited Havana, Cuba. On their return to the United States, President Truman invited Churchill to give a course of lectures at Fulton, in his home state of Missouri.

Churchill gives a press conference at the Miami Army Air Base in Florida in February 1946, before leaving for a trip to Havana, Cuba. It was his first visit to Cuba since his assignment as a war reporter some 50 years earlier.

*Churchill's youngest daughter, Mary, married
Christopher Soames, an army officer, on 11 February,
1947 at St Margaret's Westminster, where her parents
had wed nearly 40 years earlier.*

Churchill's speech, delivered on 5 March, was
broadcast by radio stations from coast to coast.
His message was that the United States should not
retreat into isolationism again but must remain on
the world stage and lead the democratic world in
defence of freedom and peace. War, poverty and
tyranny were cankers in society that had to be
expunged and the focus of Churchill's warning
was communist Russia.

'From Stettin in the Baltic to Trieste in the
Adriatic,' Churchill told his audience of
distinguished academics, 'an iron curtain has
descended across the continent (of Europe). Behind
that line lie all the capitals of the ancient states of
Central and Eastern Europe, Warsaw, Berlin,
Prague, Vienna, Budapest, Belgrade, Bucharest and

Sofia, all these famous cities and the populations
around them lie in what I must call the Soviet
sphere, and all are subject ... not only to Soviet
influence, but to a very high and, in many cases,
increasing measure of control from Moscow .... '

In Moscow, the Communist Party newspaper
Pravda accused Churchill of wheeling out his 'old
slanders' about Soviet expansionism. In London,
Labour Members of Parliament read into
Churchill's speech a proposal for a military
alliance between the British Commonwealth and
the United States to combat the spread of
communism. They denounced the speech as
warmongering and 'inimical to the cause of world
peace', and a motion of censure was put forward
against Churchill, signed by 93 Labour MPs.

FINANCIAL TROUBLE

Nothing came of the censure motion, but
Churchill felt obliged to issue a denial. 'I have
never asked for an Anglo-American military
alliance or a Treaty,' he declared. 'I have asked for

something different, and in a sense I asked for something more. I asked for fraternal association, free, voluntary, fraternal association. I have no doubts that it will come to pass, as surely as the Sun will rise tomorrow.'

The opposition Churchill experienced after Fulton did not deter him from making known his vision of Europe's future. Six months after his 'Iron Curtain speech', as it came to be known, Churchill made another speech at the University of Zurich in Switzerland. He warned against the horrifically destructive nature of the atomic bomb, and still hopeful for cooperation rather than confrontation, spoke of communist Russia as a potential partner in the democratic endeavours of the West. He promoted three political agendas that he felt should govern the future of the

world. Reconciliation was the underlying theme in all of them. He proposed rapport with the Soviet Union to head off conflict and thaw the Cold War, a process he felt could be accelerated by the fact that the United States possessed the atomic bomb and, as yet, the Soviets did not. He keenly promoted his idea of a 'United States of Europe' in which old hatreds could be

Churchill, wearing the uniform of an Air Commodore, was presented with the Médaille Militaire in Paris on 12 May, 1947. Clementine thought the uniform 'bogus' and wanted her husband to receive the medal in civilian clothes to underline the fact that he 'conquered in the war … as a Statesman.' For once, Churchill did not take her advice.

exchanged for friendly cooperation. Churchill's third theme was the need to restore the re-democratized Germany to a respectable place among the countries of the world.

In the autumn of 1946, Churchill ran into financial trouble – partly due to his own extravagance, partly to the often exorbitant demands of his family. Small-scale economies, such as reducing his stock of champagne and cutting down on expensive cigars, could not solve the problem. Chartwell, Churchill's much-loved country home in Kent, absorbed vast amounts of money and, not for the first time, he feared he might have to sell it. His friend, the newspaper proprietor William Ewert Berry, Lord Camrose,

> Churchill was downcast. He was convinced that after four years of extravagant Labour rule, Britain was facing economic ruin. 'I really do not see how our poor island is going to earn its living.'

came up with an idea to safeguard his home. Camrose arranged for 17 wealthy benefactors to purchase Chartwell for £50,000 – well over a million pounds at today's values – and allow the Churchill family to continue living there for a nominal rent. After Churchill's death, Chartwell would be given to the National Trust and kept as a permanent monument to him.

Churchill soon discovered a way out of his financial crisis: he resumed his former role as writer and historian, making use of his unique position as eye-witness to all the key events and personalities of the war years. He had already made a start on his war memoirs, *The Second World War*, in March 1946, which he planned to run to six volumes. The memoirs were guaranteed an avid international readership and Lord Camrose used his connections in the publishing world to sell them in the United States for an amount that brought Churchill US$1.4 million – almost £6 million in today's values.

The Second World War was a monumental task. Churchill worked on it 'ruthlessly', according to his chief assistant William Deaken. The book occupied the energies of a full-time research team and seven secretaries over a period of six years. Each volume was inscribed with the same motto, which expressed Churchill's own principle of honourable conduct: 'In war, resolution; in defeat, defiance; in victory, magnanimity; in peace, goodwill.'

Throughout the long gestation of his memoirs, Churchill also attended to his duties as Leader of the Opposition. He found it difficult to adjust to this secondary status and it was painful when he was forced to witness the granting of dominion status to India. Churchill's long-held hopes that

CHURCHILL MAKES A STATEMENT AFTER THE FIRST ATOMIC BOMB IS DROPPED ON HIROSHIMA, JAPAN, 6 AUGUST, 1945

The revelations of the secrets of Nature, long mercifully withheld from Man, should arouse the most solemn reflections in the mind and the conscience of every human being capable of comprehension. We must indeed pray that these awful agencies will be made to conduce to peace among the nations, and that instead of wreaking measureless havoc upon the entire globe, they may become a perennial fountain of world prosperity.

When Churchill travelled to the United States to confer with President Truman in March 1949, he urged the President to make public his willingness to use the atomic bomb to preserve democracy.

some form of British rule would survive in the 'Jewel in the Crown' of the British Empire were finally dashed.

HISTORY REPEATS ITSELF

Churchill was equally uncomfortable with the proposals of the Labour government in 1947 to nationalise the iron and steel industry. He opposed the nationalisation, using the issue to reinforce his dominant political theme: the spectre of socialist totalitarian rule.

'It is 41 years,' he said, 'since, as a young Liberal Minister in Mr Asquith's government, arguing against this same socialist fallacy, I said:

"The existing organisation of society is driven by one mainspring, competitive selection. It may be a very imperfect organisation of society, but it is all we have got between us and barbarism." I should now have to add totalitarianism, which indeed is only state-organised barbarism.' The plea failed and the British iron and steel industry was nationalised in 1949.

Churchill was downcast. He was convinced that after four years of extravagant Labour rule, Britain was facing economic ruin. 'I really do not see how our poor island is going to earn its living,' he told Clementine. His depression seemed to show in his conduct of affairs. After three or four years in opposition, there were rumblings among the rank and file of the Conservative Party that Churchill had lost his edge.

History appeared to be repeating itself, for it was not the first time Churchill had found himself out of favour with his party. When *The*

CHURCHILL IS ABSORBED BY HIS PAINTING WHILE ON HOLIDAY WITH CLEMENTINE IN MIAMI BEACH, FLORIDA, IN 1946. CHURCHILL MIXED PLEASURE WITH BUSINESS WHILE HE WAS IN THE UNITED STATES. HE DISCUSSED THE DISTRIBUTION OF HIS WAR MEMOIRS WITH HIS EDITOR, EMERY REEVES, AND DINED WITH PRESIDENT TRUMAN AT THE WHITE HOUSE, WHERE HE REHEARSED HIS FORTHCOMING SPEECH AT FULTON, MISSOURI.

Gathering Storm, the first volume in Churchill's *The Second World War*, was published, it produced a strong backlash from some party members. Conservatives loyal to the memory of Neville Chamberlain, who had died in 1940, objected to Churchill's treatment of the Munich crisis of 1938, which he presented as an example of gross mishandling and cowardice by the former Prime Minister.

RECONCILIATION URGED

Further divisions emerged within the Conservative Party when Churchill, a longstanding supporter of the Jewish people, insisted that the Labour Government recognise the State of Israel. After being voted into existence in the United Nations in 1947, Israel had declared independence on 15 May, 1948, but was immediately attacked by its Arab neighbours. The British government would not recognise the new state until January 1949, when Israel's survival became certain. Churchill's pro-Zionist sentiments were not well received within the Conservative Party. At a dinner given in Churchill's honour at the Savoy Hotel in London on 2 June, 1948, one of the guests present, the Conservative MP and diarist Henry 'Chips' Channon, noticed that 'His reception was tepid … gone is the rapture of yesteryear'.

Churchill was now 73 years old, but he still kept to a punishing timetable. In addition to his duties in Parliament and his work on *The Second World War*, he travelled extensively – to the United States, France and Italy – attending meetings, impromptu conferences and private talks, some of which lasted far into the night. This activity caught up with Churchill in August 1949 when he had a mild stroke. His right leg went numb, and he suffered cramp in his right arm. There were alarming repercussions: he became unable to sign his name and developed a limp. He realised that his illness could be used to strengthen the case for his retirement, which was already anticipated by younger Conservatives. Determined to keep his condition secret, he remained at Chartwell until mid October.

By the end of 1949, he had made a remarkable recovery. Sir Archibald Sinclair, one of Churchill's wartime Cabinet ministers, recalled that he was 'in grand form, as lively and incessant in his conversation as he was in Cabinet in the old days, eating, drinking and smoking as voraciously as ever'.

Churchill needed all his newfound energy to fight the approaching General Election, announced for 23 February, 1950. On the day, the Labour Party won a narrow victory but its majority was severely reduced, to a mere six seats. It seemed unlikely that Attlee's government could survive long with such a disadvantage. Despite being hampered by increasing deafness, Churchill flung himself into the political fray with energy and vigour in a deliberate attempt to defuse the

CHURCHILL ON THE SURRENDER OF JAPAN, 15 AUGUST, 1945

This crowning deliverance from the long and anxious years of danger and carnage should rightly be celebrated by Parliament in accordance with custom and tradition … once again, the British Commonwealth and Empire emerges safe, undiminished and united from a mortal struggle. Monstrous tyrannies which menaced our life have been beaten to the ground in ruin, and a brighter radiance illumines the Imperial Crown than any which our annals record. The light is brighter because it comes not only from the fierce but fading glare of military achievements such as an endless succession of conquerors have known, but because there mingle with it in mellow splendour the hopes, joys and blessings of almost all Mankind. This is the true glory and long will it gleam upon our forward path.

rumours that his time was past. Harold Macmillan wrote: 'Conscious that many people feel he is too old to form a Government and that this will probably be used as a cry against him at the (next) election, he has used these days to give a demonstration of energy and vitality. He has voted in every division, made a series of brilliant little speeches; shown all his qualities of humour and sarcasm and crowned all by a remarkable breakfast … of eggs, bacon, sausages and coffee, followed by

Churchill tours his constituency in February 1950. The continuing influence of his wartime speeches is evident from the posters behind him, calling him 'The Voice of Britain'. Seventeen months later, Churchill was back in power.

a large whisky and soda and a huge cigar. This latter feat commanded general admiration.'

The workload was heavy, but Churchill was fortified by his faith in the future that lay ahead of him. 'He had this premonition,' wrote his secretary Jane Portal, 'that he would be Prime Minister after the next election …. He talked about it all the time.' By the late summer of 1951, the Labour government was scraping through debates by majorities of only six or eight votes, sometimes surviving only with the help of Liberal MPs. Prime Minister Attlee was forced to announce another election for 25 October, 1951 and the result was 321 seats for the Conservatives to 295 for Labour. On the evening of 26 October, Churchill went to Buckingham Palace where, once again, the king asked him to form a government.

TWILIGHT

IN HIS SECOND TERM AS PRIME MINISTER, CHURCHILL'S CHIEF
PREOCCUPATION WAS TO RECONCILE THE TWO COLD WAR RIVALS,
THE US AND THE SOVIET UNION. HE FAILED, AND IN 1955 HAD
TO YIELD TO LONGSTANDING DEMANDS FOR HIS RESIGNATION.
CHURCHILL SPENT THE NEXT TEN YEARS UNTIL HIS
DEATH HONOURED, LAUDED AND APPLAUDED. HIS
FUNERAL IN 1965 WAS A STATE OCCASION.

WINSTON CHURCHILL BEGAN his second term of
office as Prime Minister at a pace many of his colleagues,
and his wife Clementine, were not sure he could sustain.
Once his new administration had settled in, he set off for
America on the last day of 1951 to attend talks with
President Truman. In five gruelling sessions, discussions
ranged over the threat from the Soviet Union, the
possible use of the atomic bomb, the functions of the
North Atlantic Treaty Organisation (NATO) – the
military alliance created in 1949 to defend western Europe against
aggression by the Soviet Union – and the thorny problem of peace in
the Middle East. In between sessions, Churchill travelled to Ottawa to
make a speech at a dinner given in his honour by the Canadian
government, then returned to Washington to address the US Congress.

After four demanding weeks, Churchill was tired. 'The two
speeches,' Churchill wrote to Clementine, 'were very hard and
exacting ordeals.' After the rigours of the tour, Churchill needed
two days' rest in New York before embarking for home on the
liner *Queen Mary*.

*Churchill's funeral procession (left) included a parade of
servicemen from all the battalions in which he had served.
The soldiers bearing his coffin were Grenadier Guards, the
regiment with which he had fought during World War I.
At the age of 89, Churchill was becoming increasingly frail.
Three days before the above picture was taken, he had made
his last appearance in the Commons, on 27 July, 1964.*

Just over a week after he arrived in Britain, George VI died on 6 February and, as Prime Minister, Churchill led the nation in mourning the valiant wartime monarch. Clementine feared that the strain this responsibility would put on Churchill might prove too great for him. Her fears were confirmed when Churchill suffered a minor arterial spasm that might have been the precursor to another stroke. The danger receded but neither she nor Churchill's doctor, Lord Moran, could persuade him to reduce the pressure of his overactive lifestyle.

ZEST DIMINISHED

Churchill was not yet willing to consider retirement. He knew what he wanted to achieve as Prime Minister and confided his intentions to John Colville, who was now his Joint Principal Private Secretary. Colville recalled: 'He just wanted to have time to re-establish the intimate relationship with the United States, which had been the keystone of his policy in the war, and to restore at home the liberties that had been eroded by wartime restrictions and postwar socialist measures.'

Churchill's mandate to push his policies through Parliament relied on a slim majority of only 17 seats, which made the Conservatives vulnerable to attack from the Opposition benches. In the spring of 1952 the Labour Party started to play dirty, hoping to unbalance the

When Churchill travelled to the United States early in 1952, he was entertained aboard the presidential yacht Williamsburg *by Truman. He came to respect the gutsy, forthright Truman who was much like himself – defiant in the face of adversity and unafraid of tackling controversial issues.*

During his trip to North America in 1952, Churchill travelled to Canada where he arrived on 14 January to be greeted by a 19-gun salute, cheering crowds and an honour guard of Royal Canadian Mounted Police.

government. They held a series of sessions late at night and sometimes lasting into the early hours, which were designed to tire the Conservatives and, in particular, Churchill.

'Could there be any more nauseating performance,' Chips Channon wrote in his diary on 9 April, 'than that of half a dozen hale young Socialists howling at Mr Churchill, jeering at his pronouncements and even at his entrances and exits to the House, taunting him with his advanced age and growing deafness?'

These were not Churchill's only problems. He was finding it difficult to follow the intricacies of Cabinet business and to absorb the huge amount of material generated by the meetings over which he presided. He was aware of his failing powers and became depressed and bewildered. He told Colville, 'The zest is diminished'. On 23 June, he was informed that four senior members of his government had met in secret and decided that the Prime Minister must either resign immediately or name a date when he would step down. 'There is a move to get me out,' Churchill told Lord Moran.

A NEW US PRESIDENT
Despite this gloomy news, Churchill was determined to fight back. He summoned up his vigour and formidable powers of intellect to defend his government's policies from Labour attacks in the Commons and to dominate proceedings in the Cabinet.

Churchill appeared to be in fine form when he spoke to the Conservative Conference on 10 October, 1953. Yet only three weeks earlier he was in the depths of despair, brooding on whether or not to resign as Prime Minister.

increase the possibility of international strife. Churchill's worries reinforced his desire to reconcile the two great superpowers, the United States and Soviet Russia.

To press upon President Eisenhower the importance of a reconciliation, Churchill embarked on another visit to the United States, the second of four he made in his second term as Prime Minister. He arrived in New York onboard the *Queen Mary* on 5 January, 1953. But despite several hours of intense discussion, Churchill failed to persuade Eisenhower to meet Stalin. Two months later, on 5 March, Stalin died. Eisenhower also refused to meet Stalin's successor, Georgi Malenkov, fearing that it might give Malenkov's government a propaganda coup. All Churchill's efforts to make him change his mind failed.

On 4 November, 1952, General Dwight D Eisenhower was elected President of the United States. Churchill's relationships with Eisenhower's predecessors, Roosevelt and Truman, had been cordial and there was much common ground between them. But Eisenhower had never impressed Churchill and he feared that the election of a former general as President would

THE STRAIN BEGINS TO SHOW

In Britain, Anthony Eden, Churchill's Foreign Secretary and his heir apparent, was becoming more and more restive about his prospects of being Prime Minister. Eden had hoped to succeed Churchill in 1945 but seven years later he was no nearer his goal. Eden was by then married to

CHURCHILL ENVISIONS A UNITED STATES OF EUROPE, 19 SEPTEMBER, 1946

The first step to the re-creation of the European family must be a partnership between France and Germany. In this way only can France recover the moral leadership of Europe .... The structure of the United States of Europe, if [it is] well and truly built, will be such as to make the material strength of a single state less important. Small nations will count as much as large ones and gain their honour by their contribution to the common cause .... Great Britain, the British Commonwealth of Nations, mighty America and I trust Soviet Russia – for then indeed all would be well – must be the friends and sponsors of the new Europe and must champion its right to live and shine.

Clarissa, Churchill's niece. Perhaps emboldened by the family connection, he had confronted Churchill at Chequers before his visit to the United States and asked point blank when he intended to resign. To his great frustration, Churchill refused to give him an answer. In despair, Eden told Sir Evelyn Shuckburgh, the Assistant Under Secretary of State at the Foreign Office, that he did not 'think the Old Man will ever go'.

Then, in April 1953, Eden fell gravely ill after a botched operation. A further operation almost killed him and he had to fly to the United States for corrective surgery. Once before, when Eden was suffering from jaundice, Churchill had taken over his duties at the Foreign Office. In 1953, he did so again but provoked strong objections with a speech he made in the Commons on 11 May. Churchill was once more pushing for a conference with the Soviets and told the House that even if 'no hard and fast agreements would be reached … there might be a general feeling among those gathered together that they might do something

At Elizabeth II's coronation on 2 June, 1953, Churchill was dressed as a Knight of the Garter, an honour recently conferred on him by the Queen. Churchill had been offered a peerage but refused because he wished to remain in the House of Commons and a peerage would have obliged him to sit in the House of Lords.

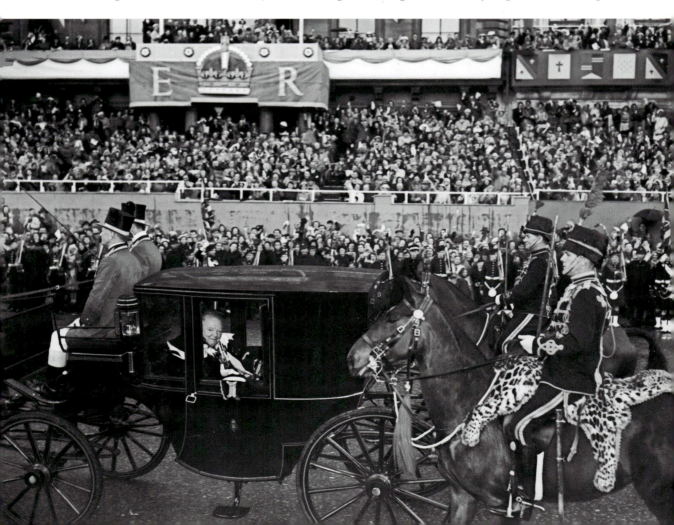

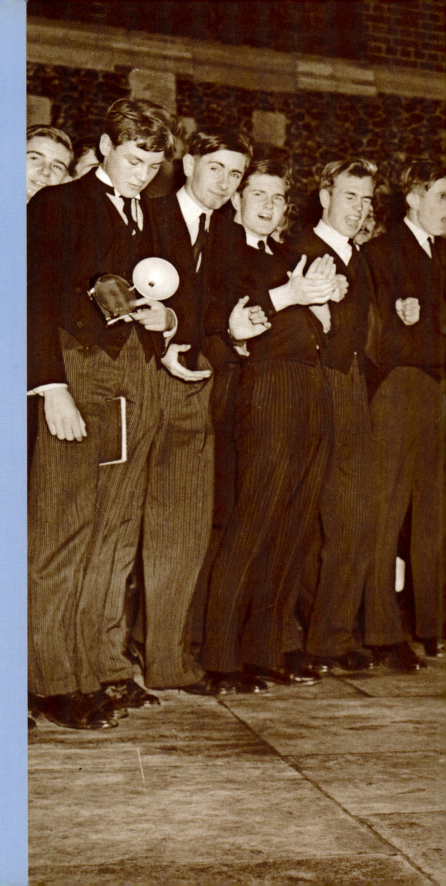

On 27 November, 1952, Churchill made his customary yearly visit to his old school, Harrow. Although he had not enjoyed his school years, he was a staunch supporter of the public school system of education, and returned to Harrow out of duty. In 1930, 35 years after he left Harrow for Sandhurst, Churchill had remarked: 'I am all for the Public Schools, but I do not want to go there again.'

better than tear the human race, including themselves, to bits.'

Some at the Foreign Office were worried that Churchill's overtures to Russia might deter the Europeans from developing stronger bonds between them, and Anthony Eden became enraged at what he regarded as Churchill's meddling with Britain's foreign policy.

The controversy arose at a busy time for Churchill. The coronation of the new monarch, Elizabeth II, and the attendant celebrations took place on 2 June. The Queen used the occasion to

honour the inspirational wartime Prime Minister by inviting Churchill to become a member of the Order of the Garter, the oldest and most prestigious of British orders of chivalry, dating back to 1348. Churchill accepted the knighthood because, as he said, he thought the Queen was 'so splendid'. In doing so, he became one of the 24 Garter knights, which entitled him to be known as Sir Winston.

But the ceremonies took their toll. Churchill was so tired that he left the royal procession as it returned to Buckingham Palace, heading for the Prime Minister's residence at 10 Downing Street. Over the next two weeks, he chaired three meetings of the British Commonwealth Prime Ministers, hosted a Foreign Office banquet for the Queen and finalised plans for a conference in Bermuda, where

Churchill arrives at Kindley Airfield in Bermuda on 2 December, 1953 for a conference to discuss the Soviet Union and its communist aims.

Churchill is accompanied by his grandson, Nicholas Soames, at the christening of Nicholas' sister, Charlotte Clementine, at Westerham Parish Church, Kent, on 6 November, 1954.

he hoped to persuade the Americans and the French to enter into talks with the Soviets.

SECOND STROKE

The strain on Churchill was becoming apparent. On 20 June, he gave a dinner at 10 Downing Street in honour of the Italian Prime Minister, Alcide de Gasperi, but just as he was leaving the dining room, he turned ghastly pale and collapsed into a chair. It was a second stroke, much more serious than the first. Churchill's mouth drooped, his left side was partially paralysed and he was unable to use his left arm. The Bermuda Conference was postponed and a press statement issued saying that the Prime Minister was in need of a complete rest, although no mention was made of the reason.

This second stroke, like the first, was kept secret. As before, it would take all of Churchill's resilience and determination to make a full and speedy recovery. Within a week, he decided to get out of his wheelchair and stand up. Gripping the sides of his chair, sweating profusely with the effort, he hauled himself to his feet, stood for a few seconds, then sat down and casually picked up his cigar. Four days later, he was able to walk short distances unaided. Two days after that, Churchill was receiving visitors and discussing Foreign Office business.

By 17 July, Churchill was once more putting pressure on Eisenhower to meet with the Soviets. When Eisenhower continued to resist, Churchill told John Colville that he considered the President 'weak and stupid'. The chances of holding a summit with the Soviets faded further when Anthony Eden returned from the United States. Eden was no more interested in a Soviet summit than Eisenhower. He believed that NATO, with its membership of 14 nations – the United States and 13 European countries – had already weakened the Soviet Union sufficiently.

Churchill appeared to have made another amazing recovery, and only eight weeks after his stroke was regularly chairing Cabinet meetings, visiting the royal family at Balmoral in Scotland, and attending the races at Doncaster. Churchill was still writing *The Second World War*, for which he was awarded the Nobel Prize for Literature in 1953. He was also working on another project, begun 20 years earlier but never published: *The History of the English-Speaking Peoples*.

Despite all these activities and achievements, there was a worn-out, rapidly deteriorating old man behind the facade. 'I am sad about Papa,' Clementine wrote to Mary on 5 September, 'because in spite of the brave show he makes, he gets very easily tired and then he gets depressed. He does too much work and has not yet learned how and when to stop.'

Churchill was well aware of the realities of his situation. He was still under pressure to resign and Anthony Eden made no secret of his desire to succeed him. Yet as long as the Soviet problem remained unresolved Churchill was reluctant to go.

DEMANDS FOR RESIGNATION

At a conference in Bermuda towards the end of 1953, Churchill was again unable to win over the Americans to his vision of a *détente*, or thawing of tension, with Soviet Russia. The French, who also took part, were not convinced

'[For] the first time I realised how much his powers had waned. In days gone by, he would have put aside his notes and devastated the opposition because he had the strongest case.'

either. A few weeks later, early in February 1954, the Soviets proved equally obdurate at a meeting of Foreign Ministers held in Berlin. Churchill was once again the voice in the wilderness. No one seemed willing to heed his message that a confrontation between east and west – the Cold War that was to last almost to the end of the 20th century – could be avoided if effort and goodwill were devoted to the task.

The demands for Churchill to step down were becoming clamorous. In February 1954 the *Daily Mirror* newspaper and *Punch* magazine called for his resignation. In March Eden became exasperated at Churchill's ceaseless efforts to persuade President Eisenhower to talk to the Soviets. The Prime Minister, he claimed, was undermining his authority as Foreign Secretary. 'This simply cannot go on!' Eden fulminated. 'He is gaga, he cannot finish his sentences ....'

DOGGED DETERMINATION

Eden was overstating the case, but Churchill's powers were undoubtedly in decline. On 5 April, while he was speaking in the Commons, a roar of 'Resign! Resign!' erupted from the Labour Party benches. Churchill did not seem to notice. As one of his Private Secretaries, Anthony Browne, commented, this was entirely out of character. '[For] the first time,' Browne remembered, ' ... I realised how much his powers had waned. In days gone by, he would have put aside his notes and devastated the opposition because he had the strongest case.' Instead he doggedly ploughed on through his speech. Churchill, the diplomat and writer Sir Evelyn Shuckburgh concluded, had 'exposed his aged feebleness to the House'.

CHURCHILL ON THE PROSPECT OF THE SOVIET UNION ACQUIRING THE ATOMIC BOMB, 9 OCTOBER, 1948

Nothing stands between Europe today and complete subjugation to Communist tyranny but the atomic bomb in American possession .... The question is asked: What will happen when they get the atom bomb themselves? .... You can judge yourself what will happen then by what is happening now. If they continue month after month disturbing and tormenting the world ... what will they do when they themselves have large quantities of atomic bombs? ... Instead of being a sombre guarantee of peace and freedom, it would have become an irresistible method of human enslavement. No one in his senses can believe that we have a limitless period of time before us .... The Western nations will be far more likely to reach a lasting settlement without bloodshed, if they formulate their just demands while they have the atomic power and before the Russian Communists have got it, too.

Despite the efforts to force him out, Churchill stubbornly clung on to his post. At Eden's urging, he made a commitment to leave office in September 1954, then changed his mind. In August, he told Eden that he would stand down in a year's time, but then informed Harold Macmillan that he meant to stay until the General Election, which was likely to take place in November 1955.

willing to talk with the Soviets. But the summit came to nothing when on 16 March, 1955 Churchill was told that neither the President nor his anti-Soviet Secretary of State, John Foster Dulles, were prepared to negotiate. Neither, it appeared, were the Soviets: on 30 March, their new leader, Malenkov's successor Nikolai Bulganin, slammed the door on a top-level conference, citing American hostility.

FINAL CRUNCH

The denouement came in the spring of 1955. In March, Churchill promised Eden, in secret, that he would resign on 5 April. Five days later, on 13 March, he withdrew his promise, encouraged by the chance of attending an Anglo-American conference in London to explore the possibilities of reducing Cold War tensions. At a meeting with Churchill the previous year, in June 1954, President Eisenhower had indicated that he was finally

This official portrait marked Churchill's 80th birthday. Although not the oldest Prime Minister, he had the longest continuous service as an MP, for which he inherited the title of Father of the House in 1964.

On 17 February, 1956, Lady Churchill (left) departed on a voyage to Ceylon (Sri Lanka) to recuperate after a bout of illness. Clementine's health had often given Churchill cause for concern, and her later years were plagued by illness.

Churchill and Clementine (above) celebrated their golden wedding anniversary on 12 September, 1958 at Cap d'Ail on the French Riviera with their son Randolph (left) and Arabella, his nine-year-old daughter from his second marriage to June Osborne.

It was the end. On 4 April, Churchill and Clementine hosted a farewell dinner at 10 Downing Street for Queen Elizabeth and her husband the Duke of Edinburgh. The next day, Churchill was driven to Buckingham Palace, where he formally handed in his resignation. Anthony Eden succeeded him as Prime Minister.

It was the end of an extraordinary and unique career, during which Churchill had held almost every high office Parliament had to offer. In nearly 50 years in and out of power, he had known success and setback, odium and adulation. The jewel in the crown of his achievement was the five years of his wartime leadership when he ensured the survival and triumph of his country and the democratic principles he held so dear.

BACKBENCH MP

Retirement proved more pleasurable than Churchill might have imagined. 'I have at the moment the great desire to stay put and do nothing,' he wrote to his American friend Bernard Baruch in late May 1955. Politics, which had been an all-consuming occupation for over half a century, faded into the background of his new life. Now his sole participation in Parliament was that of a backbench MP, although he was a backbencher with uncommon privileges. He corresponded with President Eisenhower. From time to time, Anthony Eden sought his advice. In the General Election of May 1955, Churchill campaigned in his Woodford constituency and won his seat once again. When he attended the opening session of the new House of Commons, Churchill was given a jubilant reception. He was surrounded by his fellow MPs, cheering and waving their order papers with enthusiasm, while above the Commons chamber, there was an outburst of clapping from the public gallery.

Churchill was lauded and applauded wherever he went and honours were showered on him. In 1955 he unveiled a statue of himself in the Guildhall, London, and received the freedoms of the cities of Belfast and Londonderry in Northern Ireland. In the same year, he was given the Charlemagne Prize, an award for contributions to European unity. In 1961, Churchill was made an Honorary Citizen of the United States, the first of only five foreigners to receive the title.

Churchill continued to entertain eminent guests and celebrities at Chartwell and visitors found him still well informed about current affairs. In April 1956 he lunched with Nicolai Bulganin and his co-leader Nikita Khrushchev as guests of Anthony and

'I am being taken through a course of Monet, Manet, Cezanne and Co by my hosts who are both versed in modern painting ... '

Clarissa Eden at 10 Downing Street. The irony of the occasion was not lost on Churchill. He had failed to bring Russians and Americans to the conference table, yet here he was sitting next to Khrushchev whom he found a very sociable companion. 'The Russians,' he later told Lord Moran, 'were delighted to see me. Anthony told them I won the war!'

Churchill spent much of his retirement in the south of France, staying at La Pausa, the luxurious home of Emery Reves, the editor of *The Second World War,* and his wife Wendy. Emery and Wendy were keen art collectors and music enthusiasts, and, to his delight, gave Churchill a tour of their collections. 'I am being taken through a course of Monet, Manet, Cezanne and Co by my hosts who are both versed in modern painting,' he wrote to Clementine.

During his time in France, Churchill painted, completed the fourth and last volume of *A History of the English-Speaking Peoples,* and socialised with the rich and famous, such as Aristotle Onassis, the Greek shipowner. Churchill also hoped to find a 'Dream Villa' to buy in the south of France, but despite much searching he never found it.

Even in his retirement Churchill was unable to relax the pace of his frenetic life. There were too many flights, too many changes of scene and too much work. On 19 October, 1956, he paid the price once again. While staying at La Pausa, he

CHURCHILL ON THE BERLIN AIRLIFT, 21 JULY, 1949

I was very much struck at the way in which all Germany watched the airlift and how all Germany saw the British and American planes flying to carry food to 2.5 million Germans whom the Soviet government were trying to starve. I thought that was worth all the speeches that could have been made by all the peace leaders of Europe to turn the eyes of Germany to where her true destiny lies: namely in peaceful and honourable association with the Western democracies ....

The 87-year-old Churchill arrives back in England after breaking his thigh in a fall while on holiday in Monte Carlo. The cheery gesture was deceptive. Churchill refused to be treated in hospital in France, insisting, 'I want to die in England'. An RAF Comet aircraft was sent specially to fly him home.

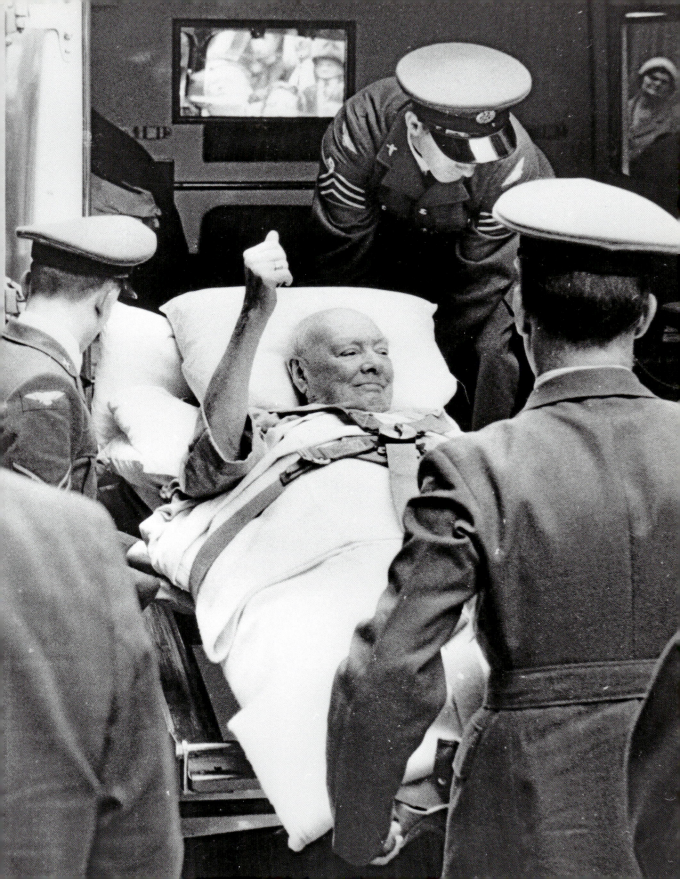

blacked out, fell to the floor and was unconscious for 20 minutes.

SUEZ CRISIS

Still extraordinarily resilient, he was sufficiently recovered by 28 October to return to Britain, where he found the country and Parliament in a furore over the Suez Crisis. The nationalisation of the Suez Canal by the Egyptian President Gamal Abdul Nasser had resulted in an invasion by British, French and Israeli troops. The Americans and Soviets strongly disapproved and forced the invaders to withdraw. 'If you had been Prime Minister, would you have done this?' John Colville asked Churchill. 'I would never have dared,' Churchill replied, 'and if I had dared, I would never have dared to stop.'

For Anthony Eden, the aftermath of Suez was painful. He was guilty of the worst solecism possible for a British Prime Minister: committing British troops to war without consulting Parliament. After waiting ten years or more to become Prime Minister, Eden's term came to a controversial and premature end. Savaged by the criticism and in poor health again, he resigned in January 1957.

VISIBLY FRAIL

In 1958, Churchill contracted pneumonia and suffered three bouts of fever. He recovered, but the experience left him visibly frail. He no longer felt capable of contributing to debates in the House of Commons. In 1958, 1959 and 1963 he suffered strokes, all of them forunately mild, but a fall he suffered in Monte Carlo in 1962 was more serious. Churchill broke his hip but refused to be hospitalized in France. A Royal Air Force Comet aircraft flew him home and as he was taken off, he gave his wartime V-sign to bystanders.

On the eve of his 90th birthday, 30 November, 1964, Churchill was greeted by a large crowd which had gathered outside his home in Hyde Park Gate, London, to sing 'For he's a jolly good fellow.'

Despite this display of fighting spirit, old age was fast overtaking Churchill. 'He does not say much now,' Harold MacMillan, Eden's successor as Prime Minister, wrote in his diary. 'For the first time, he listens. All this is rather sad, for the fight has gone out of him.'

In October 1963, Churchill's eldest daughter Diana committed suicide after two failed marriages, several nervous breakdowns and long periods of depression. It fell to Mary, Churchill's youngest daughter, to tell her father. 'The lethargy of extreme old age dulls many sensibilities,' she wrote later, 'and my father only took in slowly what I had to tell him, but then he withdrew into a great and distant silence.'

A NATION MOURNS

Churchill made his last appearance in the House of Commons, on 27 July, 1964, in a wheelchair. To those close to him, it was clear that his spark had finally gone. On 10 January, 1965, Churchill suffered his last and most serious stroke. He died on 24 January, surrounded by his three surviving children, and with Clementine holding his hand.

After Churchill's funeral, his coffin was put aboard the barge Havengore *at Tower Pier and transported along the Thames. Giant cranes by the riverside dipped in homage as the great man passed by.*

Tributes poured in from around the world: Pope Paul VI called him the 'indefatigable champion of freedom' and Queen Elizabeth II described him as 'the greatest Englishman of our time'.

Churchill was given a state funeral – the first for a commoner since that of the Duke of Wellington in 1852. Plans for it had been drawn up years earlier, and were meticulous. The entire service was broadcast on television and relayed to viewers worldwide, 350 million of them in Europe alone. Some 300,000 mourners filed past the flag-draped coffin over the three days he lay in state in Westminster Hall, the most ancient and historic part of the Houses of Parliament. At the funeral service held in St Paul's Cathedral, the 6000 mourners included Queen Elizabeth – an unprecedented appearance for a monarch, who by tradition only attends royal funerals. Five other monarchs, 15 heads of state, and representatives of 89 other nations attended the service, which ended with a trumpeter high up in the Cathedral's Whispering Gallery playing the Last Post and Reveille, the traditional trumpet call at a soldier's funeral. Afterwards, when the coffin was borne on a gun carriage through the streets of London, the watching crowds, men and women alike, were in tears.

The coffin was taken to Tower Pier on the River Thames, where it was placed on a barge and transported to Festival Pier. Then from Waterloo station, the funeral train headed out into the Oxfordshire countryside, on the journey to the churchyard at Bladon, where Churchill was buried next to his parents and his younger brother John, who had died in 1947. It was a homecoming for Churchill: close by, within sight of the graves, stood Blenheim Palace, Churchill's birthplace, magnificent in its 18th-century splendour.

EPILOGUE

In 2002, nearly 40 years after his death, Churchill was voted the greatest Briton of all time in a poll conducted by the British Broadcasting Corporation (BBC). Despite all his mistakes, despite his arrogance and his eccentricities, and despite the hatreds he roused among Conservatives and Labour alike, Churchill's reputation has survived virtually unscathed.

Two generations on, the mainstays of Churchill's life and politics retain an enduring appeal. His stubborn defiance in the face of adversity, his faith in Britain's ultimate victory, and his stirring wartime speeches inspired the nation to keep on fighting through the dark days of World War II. Churchill's heroic spirit still resonates today. As do his hatred of tyranny, persecution and intolerance, and his devotion to democratic freedom and human rights.

Churchill's son Randolph pinpointed the essence of his father's greatness and his place in history when he wrote to him after his resignation in 1955: 'Power must pass and vanish. Glory, which is achieved through a just exercise of power – which itself is accumulated by genius, toil, courage and self-sacrifice – alone remains. Your glory is enshrined for ever on the unperishable plinth of your achievement …. It will flow with the centuries.'

The gravestone of Sir Winston and Lady Churchill (who died in 1977) lies in the churchyard at Bladon in Oxfordshire. After the state funeral in London, Churchill's burial at Bladon was a quiet and private affair.

INDEX

PICTURE CREDITS

Art-Tech/MARS: 136, 139, 153, 171, 188, 192, 203
Corbis: 10, 19, 24, 38, 133, 152, 157, 174, 176, 184, 187, 200–201, 202, 204, 225, 235, 245
Mary Evans Picture Library: 37, 52, 54, 63, 64, 69
Getty Images: f/c, b/c (r), 6, 8, 9, 12, 13, 14, 17, 20, 23, 26–27, 29, 30, 33, 39, 40–41, 42, 44, 45, 47, 48–49, 50, 51, 53, 56, 58, 60–61, 62, 65, 66–67, 70, 72, 73, 75, 76–77, 79, 80, 82, 84, 85, 86–87, 89, 90, 91, 92, 93, 95, 97, 98–99, 100, 101, 102, 104, 105, 106, 109, 110–111, 112, 114, 116, 118–119, 120, 121, 123, 125, 126, 128, 130, 131, 133, 134, 135, 140–141, 142, 143, 144, 146, 149, 150–151, 154, 156, 158, 163, 165, 166–167, 169, 170, 173, 175, 177, 179, 180–181, 183, 186, 190, 191, 207, 210–211, 212, 213, 214, 215, 216, 217, 218, 219, 220, 221, 222, 223, 226, 227, 229, 230–231, 233, 234, 236, 237, 238, 239, 240–241, 242, 243, 246, 247, 249, 250–251, 252
Mirrorpix: 11, 36, 96, 115
Popperfoto: 31, 35, 46, 108, 168, 195, 253
Rex Features: 194
Topfoto: 155
TRH Pictures: b/c (l), 7, 15, 18, 28, 32, 71, 124, 127, 137, 160–161, 172, 182, 196–197, 199, 208, 209
U.S. Department of Defense: 162